JAMES MARTIN
THE GREAT BRITISH VILLAGE SHOW
COOKBOOK

A 12 Yard production for the BBC

Editor Elizabeth Watson
Senior Art Editor Sara Robin
Executive Managing Editor Adèle Hayward
Managing Art Editor Nick Harris
DTP Designer Traci Salter
Senior Jacket Creative Nicola Powling
Production Controller Luca Frassinetti
Art Director Peter Luff
Publisher Stephanie Jackson

Designer Rebecca Painter
Editor Norma MacMillan

Photography Simon Wheeler

First published in Great Britain in 2007
by Dorling Kindersley Limited,
80 Strand, London, WC2R 0RL

A Penguin Company

2 4 6 8 10 9 7 5 3 1

The Great British Village Show logo copyright © 12 Yard
Productions Ltd. 2006; The Great British Village Show
logo designed by Resolution Graphics

By arrangement with 12 Yard Productions Ltd.
12 Yard logo © 12 Yard Productions Ltd 2001
The 12 Yard logo and The Great British Village Show logo
are registered trademarks of 12 Yard Productions Ltd.
and are used under licence.

By arrangement with the BBC
BBC logo © BBC 1996
The BBC logo is a registered trademark of the British
Broadcasting Corporation and is used under licence.

A CIP catalogue record for this books is available from
The British Library

ISBN 978 1 4053 2080 1

Printed by Mohn in Germany

See our complete catalogue at **www.dk.com**

Oven temperatures
All of James's recipes have been tested in a fan-
assisted oven. In the recipes, temperatures for
cooking in a conventional oven, both electric and gas,
are also given. If you are using a conventional oven,
double check these equivalent temperatures in your
manufacturer's handbook.

contents

introduction

It's not just the produce that makes village shows up and down the country so special; it's the people, their stories, their personalities, and their quirkiness. The ladies in the WI stalls selling the delicious goods they've been making for years… The man selling handmade walking sticks with tops in the shape of fish or with a built-in whistle to attract man's best friend… Tombolas, hook a duck, and wellie wanging… Honey farmers… Knitting stalls with their quilts and toilet roll covers (in what other country in the world would you see a Barbie doll cut in half, with a knitted skirt stitched onto her backside and stuffed over a bog roll?). All this and the rest of the amazing stuff is what makes the village shows here so special.

Don't get me wrong, I'm not taking the mick. I love them. What's great about everything on offer is that it's made and produced by people who really care about what they do. How else could you explain why someone would spend up to a year growing massive long carrots in drainpipes down the side of their house, just for a rosette and 30 quid if they win? Or growing 300 perfect shallots to find just nine to place on show, all the same size so they can fit through the judges' 30mm (1 ¼in) ring? The Great British Village Show series took the institution of the village show to a national level. Six regional heats took place in some of the most beautiful stately homes of Great Britain, with each heat consisting of 15 categories. The winner of each class went through to take part in the final competition at Highgrove. At the final, the giant marrows and pumpkins were so huge, it took seven big Army boys to lift them off the trucks.

Talking of Highgrove, I'd like to thank Their Royal Highnesses The Prince of Wales and the Duchess of Cornwall for allowing us to take over their house for the final. I think, like me, they couldn't believe the quality of the produce on offer. This was the first time I had seen impressive vegetables like this. As a chef I felt a bit embarrassed at first that I knew nothing about what the competitors were doing. Of course, if I'd been given a pot and some butter, I'd have been on my way.

Of all the stalls at the shows, the one that made the most money from me was the WI stall. The range of cakes, jams, and chutneys proudly displayed on their trestle tables, all individually priced and labelled with the maker's name on the side, was irresistible to me. I just love the way the amazing ladies stand behind the doilied plates with their aprons on and an old biscuit tin full of change. There are no additives or fancy colourings used here, unlike the supermarket shelves with cakes and biscuits designed to attract the kids with glow-in-the-dark sweets on the top. Oh no, this is baking at its best. These are real cooks. I not only like to browse the table but also can't resist getting hints and tips on baking and jam-making from the ladies in the know. As a keen fruit and veg grower, I like to make preserves. It's the perfect way to remind you of the great summer produce you had in the garden as the nights draw in.

So what is this book all about? Well, apart from recipes using the best produce from village shows and farmers' markets, it has invaluable hints and tips from great home cooks on jam-making, how to create perfect cakes for competitions, and general cooking at home. It also has brilliant top tips from judges on how to produce prize-winning vegetables that aren't just for show – they really do taste great too. Experts offer advice on the best varieties to grow in your garden, and which fruits and vegetables are in season when.

Gardening, in particular veg and fruit gardening, has had a huge upsurge in popularity in recent years, partly due to what is available to us in the supermarkets and all the food miles wasted. But, speaking from experience, it's also because growing vegetables and fruit at home is really quite easy, and, of course, you can't even begin to compare the taste of the bagged veg with a homegrown carrot straight out of the ground. In my garden I'm not interested in fancy Latin names. Simple rules apply: tell me what seeds to buy and where from, what muck to grow them in, and when I can harvest and eat my produce, and that's it.

I think my passion for food and gardening started in a humble allotment in York with my uncle and granddad…walking into the greenhouse and tasting fresh tomatoes off the vine for the first time, and fresh fruit just picked off the tree…all those smells and tastes that you never forget as you get older. Nowadays, as we all try to get children to eat better food, what better way than to start your own veg patch at the bottom of the garden or on an allotment? If kids could only get involved in growing the produce from seeds and plants, maybe it would stop them hating the green stuff they push around their plates with the Sunday roast.

I really hope you enjoy this book. It's been a real pleasure to write and to be involved in a project that's so close to my heart, being brought up on a farm and good home cooking. So, the next time you see a village fête or show sign while driving along somewhere, pop in. You never know what you might find.

1

starters and light meals

Chilled Tomato Soup **Cream of Artichoke Soup with Pan-Fried Scallops** Smoked Salmon Potato Cakes with Crème Fraîche **Smoked Haddock Chowder** Celeriac Salad with Lemon and Rosemary Roast Salmon **Salad Niçoise with Seared Sea Bass** Smoked Trout and Rhubarb Salad with Elderflower Dressing **Whole Poached Salmon** Poached Salmon with Nasturtium and Leaf Salad, and Onion Salsa **Herbed Kipper Pâté** Smoked Salmon, Prawn, and Herb Pies **Potted Duck and Pork** Celery Waldorf Salad with Chicken Breast **Chicory, Walnut, and Baby Beetroot Salad with Stilton Dressing** Savoy Cabbage Salad with Prosciutto and Parmesan **Broad Bean and Artichoke Salad** Carrot Salad with Orange and Orange-Blossom Water **Twice-Baked Goat's Cheese Soufflé with Apple and Walnut Salad** Roast Pumpkin and Parmesan Soufflé **Pork and Chicken Liver Terrine** Fab Cheesy Garlic Bread **Yorkshire Rarebit** Salmon, Cherry Tomato, and Pea Frittata **Bacon, Cheese, and Tomato Quiche** Bridies **Roast Pumpkin and Polenta Croquettes** Tomato and Basil Sorbet **Steve Rutterford's Tomatoes in Tea**

The great thing about produce at the markets and shows is seasonality. In summer, when tomatoes are at their best and most juicy, they are perfect for using to make a soup like this. Cold soups aren't as popular as hot ones, but this is really delicious and will win you over.

CHILLED TOMATO SOUP

serves 4–6

soup
2 slices of white bread, crusts removed and torn into pieces
900ml (1½ pints) tomato juice
6 ripe plum tomatoes
1 small cucumber
1 red onion, cut into 5mm (¼ in) slices
1 red pepper, roasted, peeled, and diced
3 garlic cloves, very finely chopped
1 tbsp sherry vinegar
Tabasco sauce to taste
salt and pepper
extra virgin olive oil, to finish
torn basil leaves, to garnish

croûtons
3 tbsp olive oil
2 slices of white bread, crusts removed and cut into 1cm (½ in) cubes

1 Put the bread in a large bowl and cover with the tomato juice. Set aside to soak while you prepare the tomatoes. Plunge the tomatoes into boiling water and blanch for 20–30 seconds, then refresh them in iced water and peel off the skin. Cut the tomatoes into quarters. Strip out and discard the pips and pulp, then dice the tomato flesh into 1cm (½in) pieces.

2 Peel the skin from the cucumber in strips and cut these strips lengthways into 1cm (½in) slices. Cut the slices into strips and, finally, cut the strips into dice. Deseed the flesh, then dice it.

3 Mash the soaked bread, then add the tomatoes, cucumber skin and flesh, onion, red pepper, and garlic to the bowl and stir to mix. Add the sherry vinegar, and season with Tabasco sauce, salt, and pepper. Place in the fridge to chill for 1–2 hours.

4 To make the croûtons, season the olive oil and toss the cubes of bread in it, then fry them gently in a non-stick pan until they are nicely crisp and a good golden brown. Transfer to kitchen paper to cool.

5 Ladle the chilled soup into bowls and zig-zag the tops with some extra virgin olive oil. Garnish with the croûtons and some torn basil leaves.

tip   You can roast and peel the pepper yourself, or use those bought in a jar.

In The Great British Village Show the schedule for the tomato class required 6 medium sized tomatoes (roughly 65mm in diameter). Each tomato had to have its calyx and an inch of stem attached. Both indoor and outdoor tomatoes were judged in the same class.

THE TOMATO CLASS

Head Judge Medwyn Williams
"The judges look for well grown fruits, uniform in size, shape, and colour, which are ripe, yet firm, have fresh calyces and natural bloom, and are free from blemishes."

Judge John Trim
"When selecting tomatoes for competition, choose fruits with unblemished skins, no soft spots or bruising, and ones that are free of pest or disease damage."

Judge Gerald Treweek
"To grow your own tomatoes, sow them in the greenhouse at 70°F using a seed compost. Prick out when ready and pot on. Set the plants out into 3-gallon buckets with a 50/50 mixture of John Junes No.3 and Multipurpose. This way you can regulate the feed. Feed the plants with a soluble tomato fertilizer when the first truss sets. Only grow 6 tomatoes per truss."

Charles Maisey at The Great British Village Show at Dyffryn Gardens

There are two types of artichoke, globe and jerusalem. The first looks like a flower and the other a root, like ginger — it's the latter type I use for this creamy soup. Jerusalem artichokes need to be used fast after peeling as they go brown very quickly.

CREAM OF ARTICHOKE SOUP WITH PAN-FRIED SCALLOPS

serves 4

2 tbsp olive oil
250g (9oz) Jerusalem
  artichokes, peeled and diced
1 medium potato, Desiree
  or King Edward, peeled
  and diced
2 shallots, sliced
1 garlic clove, chopped
2 sprigs of fresh thyme
4 tbsp white wine
1 litre (1¾ pints) vegetable
  stock
5 tbsp double cream
salt and pepper
8 scallops, removed from
  shells
knob of butter

1 Heat 1 tbsp of the olive oil in a large pan and sweat the artichokes, potato, and shallots with the garlic and thyme for a few minutes to soften, without colouring. Stir in the white wine and allow to reduce by half. Pour in the vegetable stock and bring to the boil. Reduce the heat and simmer for 10–15 minutes until the vegetables are tender.

2 Stir in the cream and bring to the boil. Remove from the heat and allow to cool slightly, then remove the thyme. Purée in a blender, in batches as necessary. Return to the pan and season to taste. Reheat if necessary and keep warm.

3 For the scallops, heat the remaining oil in a frying pan and fry the scallops for 1–2 minutes until they are golden brown on the underside. Turn them over, add a knob of butter to the pan, and cook for a further 1–2 minutes, basting with the butter. Remove from the pan.

4 To serve, divide the soup among warmed bowls and garnish each with two scallops.

tip   To create a lighter soup, just before serving, stir 4 tbsp milk into the soup and blitz with a hand blender until foaming. Serve straightaway.

This dish is great for lunch as well as breakfast. Potato cakes, which are called rösti in Switzerland, can sometimes be too greasy, but adding crème fraîche to the grated potatoes makes the cakes more moist than usual and they taste better.

SMOKED SALMON POTATO CAKES WITH CRÈME FRAÎCHE

serves 2

600g (1¼lb) peeled and grated
   potatoes, preferably
   King Edwards
75g (2½oz) crème fraîche
salt and pepper
75g (2½oz) butter
125g (4½oz) sliced smoked
   salmon, cut into strips
1 tbsp chopped fresh chives

1 Preheat the oven to 200°C fan (220°C/gas 7).

2 Mix the grated potato with the crème fraîche and seasoning. Take a heavy non-stick frying pan and place on a medium heat. When the pan is hot, add a little of the butter and set two 7.5cm (3in) metal rings in the pan. Place 3–4 tbsp of the potato mixture inside each ring and press down well with the spoon. Cook, pressing the potato down firmly, for 4–5 minutes until the underside of each cake is golden brown. Turn the cakes over and cook for another 4–5 minutes until golden brown on the other side.

3 Remove from the pan and turn the cakes out of the metal rings onto a baking tray. Top the potato cakes with the smoked salmon, arranging the strips to resemble a rose. Place in the oven to cook for 8–10 minutes.

4 Melt the remaining butter in a small pan, then remove from the heat. Season and add the chopped chives.

5 Place the potato cakes on warmed plates, spoon over the chive butter, and serve

tip   Before adding the crème fraîche to the grated potatoes, squeeze them in a sieve or in a clean tea towel to remove excess moisture.

I ate the best chowder ever in Monterey, California, but also had the worst fish dish of my life there, which was steamed bass in Budweiser. It tasted awful. Although a chowder is meant to be a hearty soup, I don't like it too thick. The one here is perfect.

SMOKED HADDOCK CHOWDER

serves 4

2 tbsp olive oil
2 potatoes, such as King
   Edwards, peeled and diced
1 large leek, diced
1 onion, diced
1 garlic clove, crushed
3 sprigs of fresh thyme,
   stalks discarded
4 tbsp white wine
600ml (1 pint) fish stock
500ml (17fl oz) chicken stock
200g (7oz) undyed smoked
   haddock fillet,
   skinned and diced
1 tsp chopped fresh dill
150ml (5fl oz) double cream

1 Heat the oil in a heavy-bottomed saucepan and sweat the potatoes, leek, and onion with the garlic and thyme leaves for a few minutes, without colouring.

2 Add the white wine to the pan and allow to reduce, then add the fish stock and chicken stock and bring to the boil. Reduce the heat and simmer gently for 10–15 minutes until the potatoes are cooked.

3 Add the smoked haddock to the pan together with the dill. Bring back to the boil. Pour in the cream and return to the boil, then remove from the heat. Season to taste and serve.

tip   If you prefer a thicker consistency, take a couple of ladlefuls of the soup and purée in a blender, then add back to the rest of the soup.

Celeriac rémoulade — a simple mix of raw celeriac in a mayonnaise dressing — is a French dish that I've always loved. This is my version, served with roast salmon. It's good with chicken and grilled steak too.

CELERIAC SALAD WITH LEMON AND ROSEMARY ROAST SALMON

serves 4

salad
½ medium celeriac
4 tbsp grain mustard
8 tbsp mayonnaise
grated zest and juice of
  1 lemon
1 tbsp chopped fresh
  flat-leaf parsley
dash of Worcestershire sauce
salt and pepper
100g (3½ oz) mixed salad leaves
drizzle of balsamic vinegar
drizzle of extra virgin olive oil

salmon
30g (1oz) unsalted butter
1 tbsp olive oil
4 portions of salmon fillet,
  about 175g (6oz) each
2 lemons, cut in half
2 sprigs of fresh rosemary

1 Preheat the oven to 200°C fan (220°C/gas 7).

2 Peel the celeriac thickly. Slice it very thinly, using a mandolin or sharp knife. Then cut the slices into fine julienne (thin strips). Place in a bowl. Add the mustard, mayonnaise, lemon zest and juice, parsley, and Worcestershire sauce and mix well. Season well with salt and pepper. Set aside.

3 To cook the salmon, heat an ovenproof frying pan on a high heat. When hot, add the butter and oil. Season the salmon, then fry in the butter and oil for 2–3 minutes. Turn the salmon over and add the lemon halves and rosemary. Place the pan in the oven and roast the salmon for 3–4 minutes.

4 Serve the hot roast salmon with the celeriac, and salad leaves dressed with balsamic vinegar and olive oil.

Smoked oily fish like mackerel and trout are often served with a slightly sour fruit such as rhubarb or gooseberries. That's why chutneys go so well with dishes like this. Using rhubarb saves a lot of time.

SMOKED TROUT AND RHUBARB SALAD WITH ELDERFLOWER DRESSING

serves 4

salad
125g (4½oz) rhubarb
200g (7oz) mixed salad leaves
2 tbsp chopped fresh
    flat-leaf parsley
¼ tsp freshly grated
    horseradish
drizzle of olive oil
4 hot-smoked trout fillets

dressing
2 tbsp extra virgin olive oil
3 tbsp vegetable or
    sunflower oil
grated zest of ½ lemon
squeeze of lemon juice
1 tbsp elderflower cordial
1 tsp white wine vinegar
salt and pepper

1 Very finely slice the rhubarb using a mandoline or sharp knife. Toss the rhubarb slices with the salad leaves, parsley, grated horseradish, and olive oil in a large bowl. Flake the smoked trout, discarding any skin, and stir into the salad. Set aside until ready to serve.

2 To make the dressing, whisk together the olive and vegetable oils, the lemon zest and juice, cordial, vinegar, and seasoning in a small bowl. Pour over the salad and toss to coat all the ingredients with the dressing.

3 Divide the trout and rhubarb salad among serving plates.

Nothing captures the taste of summer better than this dish, and it's so simple to make. Don't worry if you haven't got a fish kettle for poaching the salmon — a large roasting tin can be used instead.

WHOLE POACHED SALMON

serves 12–14

1 whole salmon, 2.5-2.75kg
    (5½–6lb), scaled and gutted
1 onion, quartered
2 bay leaves
4 tbsp white wine vinegar
1 lemon, quartered
sea salt
cracked black pepper

to serve
lemon wedges
mayonnaise

1 Place the salmon in a fish kettle (or in a large roasting tin). Add enough cold water to cover the fish (it must be completely submerged). Add the onion, bay leaves, vinegar, and lemon plus a good pinch of salt and a few twists of black pepper.

2 Cover with a lid (or with foil) and bring to the boil on the stovetop. (It is easier and quicker to put the pan over two burners.) Once boiling, remove from the heat and leave the fish in the water until cool.

3 Carefully remove the salmon and place on a board. Scrape off the skin and place the fish on a large, flat serving dish. Lever off big chunks of salmon from the bone and serve with lemon wedges and a dollop of mayo. Lovely.

I have to say that I used to think flowers on dishes was a bit naff, but having tasted nasturtiums I've changed my mind. If you can't find jalapeño chillies, another type will do — I grow jalapeños at home in the garden.

POACHED SALMON WITH NASTURTIUM AND LEAF SALAD, AND ONION SALSA

serves 4

salmon
4 portions of skinless salmon
   fillet, 200g (7oz) each
salt and pepper
½ glass white wine
750ml (1¼ pints) fish stock
1 bouquet garni
juice of ½ lemon

salsa
200g (7oz) white onions,
   finely chopped
3 jalapeño chillies,
   very finely chopped
6 tbsp extra virgin olive oil
juice of 2 lemons
sea salt

salad
30g (1oz) nasturtium blossoms
50g (1¾oz) wild rocket leaves
50g (1¾oz) lamb's lettuce
3½ tbsp olive oil

1 Place the salmon fillets in a pan, season, and pour over the white wine and fish stock. Add the bouquet garni. Bring to the boil, then turn down to a simmer and cook for 3 minutes. Remove from the heat. Add the lemon juice, cover, and leave to steam for 7–8 minutes.

2 Meanwhile, to make the salsa, combine the ingredients in a bowl and mix well. Spoon onto the plates.

3 Put the nasturtium blossoms and salad leaves in a bowl, pour over the olive oil, and mix together very gently. Arrange on the plates with the salsa.

4 Remove the cooked salmon fillets from the pan, sit them on top of the salsa, and serve immediately.

The Great British Village Show
Petworth House and Park, West Sussex

Hundreds of competitors, seasoned experts and complete novices alike, flocked to The Great British Village Show regional heat at Petworth House to compete in 15 different classes in the hope of winning first prize and a place in the grand final at Highgrove. Among the hopeful entrants were pupils from St Joseph's Primary School in London, who came with their miniature gardens. And, in a world where size means everything, 6oz was all that separated two friends' entries as they battled it out in the heaviest leek class.

Here in the UK we used to eat a lot of herrings, but they are now sadly out of fashion, except pickled as rollmops or smoked to become kippers. Last year I visited a port off the west coast of Scotland where there were once 200 herring boats. Now there are none. It's such a shame. As all kipper lovers know, herring is really good.

HERBED KIPPER PÂTÉ

serves 4

4 kipper fillets, cooked and
   flaked
200g (7oz) cream cheese
1½–2 tsp chopped fresh dill
1 tbsp chopped fresh chives
¼ tsp cayenne pepper
grated zest and juice of
   ½ lemon
salt and pepper
55g (2oz) butter, melted
few sprigs of fresh dill,
   to garnish
crusty bread, to serve

1 Place the kipper pieces in a food processor and pulse briefly, to break down. Transfer to a large bowl and add the cream cheese, fresh herbs, cayenne pepper, and lemon zest and juice. Mix well. Season to taste.

2 Spoon the mixture into four greased 10cm (4in) ramekins and smooth the top. Pour the melted butter over to make a 1cm (½in) thick layer. Place a sprig of dill on each ramekin. Cover and chill for up to 2 hours until firm and set.

3 Serve with crusty bread.

Smoked salmon is delicious just as it is, but cooking brings a whole new flavour to it. These are kind of like posh fish pies. You don't have to use prawns — a mix of smoked and fresh salmon is great too.

SMOKED SALMON, PRAWN, AND HERB PIES

makes 6 pies

pastry
200g (7oz) butter
350g (12oz) plain flour, plus
    extra for dusting
pinch of salt
beaten egg to glaze

filling
200g (7oz) smoked salmon,
    chopped
250g (9oz) peeled small
    raw prawns
25g (scant 1oz) Parmesan
    cheese, freshly grated
2 tbsp chopped fresh dill
1 garlic clove, finely chopped
200g (7oz) mascarpone or
    good cream cheese
grated zest of 1 lemon
black pepper

illustrated on pages 28–29

1 Preheat the oven to 200°C fan (220°C/gas 7).

2 To make the pastry, chill the butter in the freezer for about 20 minutes until it is very hard. Sift the flour and salt into a mixing bowl. Holding the butter with the butter paper, or a piece of baking parchment or greaseproof paper, grate it into the flour, working quickly. Stir the butter and flour together, sprinkle over 6 tbsp chilled water, and mix to make a dough, adding a little more water if needed. Wrap in cling film and chill for about 30 minutes before using.

3 On a floured surface, roll out the pastry to form a large sheet 3mm (⅛in) thick. Cut out six circles of 12cm (5in) diameter and six circles of 15cm (6in) diameter.

4 Mix together the smoked salmon, prawns, Parmesan, dill, garlic, mascarpone, lemon zest, and plenty of black pepper. Dollop 2–3 tbsp of the mixture in the centre of each of the smaller pastry circles. Brush the edges of the circles with a little beaten egg. Position the larger circles on top and press the pastry edges together to seal. Crimp the edges with your fingertips. Use a sharp knife to make a small hole in the centre of each pie lid.

5 Transfer the pies to a baking tray. Brush them with a little beaten egg, then bake for about 20 minutes until golden and crisp. Serve hot or cold.

Tuna is normally used in this classic salad of French origin. But on one occasion I made the salad with French beans I'd grown in the garden and served it for dinner with a freshly caught bass. The whole lot was a winner.

SALAD NICOISE WITH SEARED SEA BASS

serves 4

dressing
½ garlic clove
2 canned anchovy fillets
1 egg yolk
juice of ½ lemon
100ml (3½fl oz) olive oil
1 tsp Dijon mustard
salt and pepper

croûtons
4 slices from a French stick,
    cut diagonally
1 garlic clove, halved
olive oil

salad
8 quail's eggs
2 handfuls of French beans
1 sea bass, about 900g (2lb),
    scaled and filleted
olive oil
10 cherry tomatoes
8 new potatoes, cooked and
    cut in half
10 black olives

1 Preheat the oven to 170°C fan (190°C/gas 5).

2 To make the dressing, place the garlic, anchovy, and egg yolk in a mortar, and pound and mix with the pestle to make a paste. Add the lemon juice, then drizzle in the olive oil while mixing well. Add the mustard and season to taste. Set aside.

3 For the croûtons, rub the slices of bread with the garlic, then place on a baking tray and drizzle over some olive oil. Bake for 5–6 minutes until golden. Leave to cool.

4 Soft boil the quail's eggs in boiling water for 2½ minutes. Lift out and place in cold water to stop the cooking. Peel the eggs and cut in half.

5 Blanch the French beans in boiling water for 2–3 minutes. Drain, refresh in iced water, and cut in half.

6 To cook the sea bass, place a non-stick frying pan on a high heat, add a little olive oil, and place the fish skin side down in the pan. Cook, holding it down to prevent it from curling up, for 2–3 minutes. Turn the fish over and cook for a further 1–2 minutes. Remove from the heat and leave the fish in the pan for 1–2 minutes to finish cooking, then lift out onto a plate.

7 Add the tomatoes to the pan and cook for a few minutes, then remove them and place on the croûtons.

8 Combine the French beans, potatoes, olives, and eggs in a bowl and mix with the dressing. Spoon onto a serving plate. Top with the sea bass and place the croûtons around the edge.

The Waldorf salad was created over a hundred years ago at the Waldorf–Astoria Hotel in New York, and it hasn't really changed much since then. I've used Russet apples in my version, but I also like Cox's as they give a nice sharpness and bite to the salad.

CELERY WALDORF SALAD WITH CHICKEN BREAST

serves 4

420g (15oz) Russet apples, cut into 5mm (¼in) dice
140g (5oz) celery, cut into 5mm (¼in) dice
70g (2½oz) walnut halves or pieces
100g (3½oz) mayonnaise
about 100g (3½oz) mixed salad leaves
¼ tsp paprika
2 tsp olive oil
4 boneless chicken breasts, skin on

1 Preheat the oven to 200°C fan (220°C/gas 7).

2 Combine the apples, celery, and walnuts in a bowl. Add the mayonnaise and mix thoroughly. Arrange the salad leaves on each plate, spoon the apple mixture on top, and dust with a little paprika. Set aside.

3 Heat a non-stick ovenproof frying pan and add the olive oil, then place the chicken breasts skin side down in the pan. Fry over a medium heat for 3–4 minutes, then turn the breasts over and cook for a further 4 minutes. Transfer the pan to the oven to roast for 10 minutes until the chicken is cooked through.

4 Remove the chicken from the oven and allow to stand for a couple of minutes, then slice the breasts and arrange on the plates next to the salad

I grow loads of beetroot at home. If you are going to cook it yourself, boil it in the skins as otherwise the beets will bleed. Beetroot and Stilton makes a great combination. I got the idea for this dressing from some cider vinegar I picked up at a village show.

CHICORY, WALNUT, AND BABY BEETROOT SALAD WITH STILTON DRESSING

serves 4

2 heads of red or green chicory
100g (3½oz) walnut pieces
100g (3½oz) mixed salad
   leaves
200g (7oz) cooked baby
   beetroot, cut in half
   or quarters

dressing
50g (1¾oz) Stilton cheese,
   broken into pieces
2 tbsp cider vinegar
4 tbsp olive oil
2 tsp warm water
salt and pepper

1 Separate the chicory leaves and put them in a large bowl. Add the walnut pieces and salad leaves and toss together. Stir in the baby beetroot.

2 For the dressing, blend all the ingredients together in a mini food processor until smooth.

3 Pour the dressing over the salad and toss gently together to coat. Divide among serving plates.

I love this salad and have it on all my restaurant menus. It's so simple. The trick is to use the best ham and olive oil you can find, and the freshest, sweetest cabbage.

SAVOY CABBAGE SALAD WITH PROSCIUTTO AND PARMESAN

serves 6

100g (3½oz) Savoy cabbage
  (the inner, paler leaves)
3½ tbsp extra virgin olive oil
sea salt and pepper
2½ tbsp balsamic vinegar
  (must be at least 4 years old)
300g (11oz) Parmesan cheese
  in one piece
24 slices of prosciutto

1 Using a large, sharp, wide-bladed knife, shave the cabbage into the finest possible shreds. Place the shreds in a bowl and add the olive oil and salt and pepper to taste. Toss together, then add the vinegar.

2 Break the Parmesan into little pieces using a pointed knife. Ease pieces away from the main piece so that they naturally separate along the crystals that form in the cheese. The pieces should be about 2–3 cm (1in) long and up to 5mm (¼in) thick. Add to the cabbage mixture and toss.

3 Arrange the slices of prosciutto over each plate and cover with two spoonfuls of the cabbage and Parmesan mixture. If you like, drizzle a little extra balsamic vinegar and extra virgin olive oil over each plate. Serve immediately.

Broad beans are one of my favourite vegetables. Like peas, they are almost as good frozen as fresh. Unless they are really young fresh beans, they do need to be skinned, which is easy to do. Just blanch them, then press gently and the bright green bean will pop out.

BROAD BEAN AND ARTICHOKE SALAD

serves 4

225g (8oz) podded broad beans
1 jar of artichokes in olive oil
225g (8oz) leftover cooked
  chicken or salmon
juice of 1 lemon
drizzle of extra virgin olive oil
salt and pepper
1 tbsp chopped fresh mint
1 tbsp chopped fresh dill

1 Blanch the broad beans in boiling water for 2–3 minutes. Drain in a colander and refresh in iced water, then slip them out of their papery skins.

2 Remove the artichoke hearts from the jar and place on a serving plate with the ripped up pieces of chicken or salmon. Sprinkle over the broad beans.

3 Whisk the lemon juice and oil with seasoning to taste. Sprinkle the herbs over the salad, then drizzle over the dressing. Check the seasoning and serve.

The Great British Village Show
Montacute House, Somerset

Montacute House, the Elizabethan house, garden, and park that was the backdrop for Emma Thompson's film *Sense and Sensibility*, made the ideal location for The Great British Village Show. Eager competitors from all over the region brought their arts and crafts, cakes and preserves, and fruit and vegetables for display, including a group of friends, the "Paignton Allotmenteers". In the runner bean class the quality of the top two entries was so close that the head judge had to be consulted. The heaviest marrow, the giant of the vegetable world, was so huge it was described as "a sleeping crocodile".

My head chef, Yuri, came up with the idea for this salad. He's from India, where they use flower waters, in particular rose water, a fair bit in their cooking. The salad was created as a garnish for grilled halibut, but goes well with other plainly cooked fish.

CARROT SALAD WITH ORANGE AND ORANGE-BLOSSOM WATER

serves 4

500g (1lb 2oz) carrots
2 juicy oranges
juice of 3 oranges
juice of 1 lemon
2 tbsp orange-blossom water
2 tbsp caster sugar
½ tsp salt
¼ tsp ground white pepper
1 tsp ground cinnamon

1 Peel the carrots and grate into a serving bowl. Carefully peel the oranges and remove the pith and pips. Cut the flesh into cubes and add to the grated carrots.

2 Mix together the orange juice, lemon juice, orange-blossom water, sugar, salt, and pepper, and pour onto the carrots and oranges. Cover with cling film and refrigerate until well chilled. Sprinkle over the cinnamon before serving.

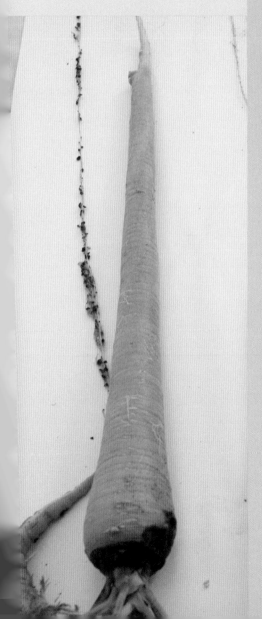

The longest carrot at the final of The Great British Village Show was an astounding 207cm (7 feet 3 inches) and was a new world record!

Growing carrots for length requires a particular dedication and competitors on The Great British Village Show grew them in 21-feet tubes resting against the walls of their houses. The carrots were covered in quilts to keep them warm, with a black outer covering to keep the heat in.

THE LONGEST CARROT

Judge Gerald Treweek
"The sweetest variety of carrot to grow is Chantenay Red Cored, 2. Sow them in the first week of April, just using a general fertilizer. Cover them to protect from carrot fly, don't thin them out, and then they should be ready to pull about the first week in July."

Judge John Trim
"Carrots like a nice, open, friable soil, with no stones. Finger-size carrots will be ready in approximately 10 weeks. For a late sowing to see me through the winter months, I sow the tasty variety Autumn King."

Head Judge Medwyn Williams
"If you haven't got space for carrots, or indeed, if you haven't got any soil whatsoever, why not grow some small carrots and Kohl Rabi in pots or Gro bags on your patio? The variety Parmex will grow easily in shallow bags and the flavour is really carroty, I love it."

Neal's Yard Perroche is one of my favourite goat's milk cheeses. It's made by Charlie Westhead of Neal's Yard Creamery in Dorstone, Herefordshire. It can be bought plain or coated in herbs. If you can't get this then any soft goat's cheese will do for this soufflé.

TWICE-BAKED GOAT'S CHEESE SOUFFLÉ WITH APPLE AND WALNUT SALAD

serves 8

soufflé
140g (5oz) unsalted butter
140g (5oz) plain flour
700ml (24fl oz) warm milk
250g (9oz) soft goat's
  cheese, mashed
2 tbsp freshly grated
  Parmesan cheese
1 tbsp Dijon mustard
1 tbsp chopped fresh
  thyme leaves
6 eggs, separated
salt and pepper

apple and walnut salad
a handful of frisée leaves
a handful of watercress or
  rocket leaves
2 red apples, thinly sliced
1 tbsp chopped fresh chives
50g (1¾oz) toasted walnuts,
  chopped
red wine vinegar
extra virgin olive oil

1 Preheat the oven to 180°C fan (200°C/gas 6).

2 Melt 15g (½oz) of the butter and use to grease eight 185ml (6½fl oz) capacity soufflé dishes. Melt the remaining butter in a large saucepan over a medium heat. Add the flour and mix well. Cook over a low heat for 5–8 minutes, stirring with a wooden spoon. Gradually add the warm milk, a little at a time, stirring constantly to avoid any lumps forming. Reduce the heat to very low and cook for another 5–8 minutes.

3 Remove from the heat and strain into a bowl. Leave to cool slightly, then stir in the goat's cheese, Parmesan, mustard, and thyme. Set aside to cool for a few minutes.

4 Beat the egg yolks into the cooled mixture and season with salt and pepper. In a clean, dry bowl, whisk the egg whites until they hold medium peaks. Use a metal spoon to fold the egg whites into the soufflé mixture.

5 Divide the mixture among the soufflé dishes and set the dishes in a roasting tin. Pour enough boiling water into the tin to reach halfway up the sides of the dishes. Bake the soufflés for 15–20 minutes until risen and evenly coloured. Remove the dishes from the tin and cool for 10 minutes. Leave the oven on, and preheat the grill to medium.

parmesan glaze
125ml (4fl oz) double cream
60g (2¼oz) Parmesan cheese,
 freshly grated
2 egg yolks

6 While the soufflés are cooling, make the apple and walnut salad. Toss together the frisée, watercress, apples, chives, and walnuts. Add a splash of red wine vinegar, a good drizzle of olive oil, and a seasoning of salt and pepper. Set aside.

7 Run a knife around the edge of each soufflé, then turn it out onto a wire rack. Using a palette knife, transfer the soufflés, still upside down, to a baking tray lined with baking parchment and bake for 10 minutes.

8 Meanwhile, make the Parmesan glaze by whisking together the cream, Parmesan, and egg yolks until combined. Coat the tops of the soufflés with the Parmesan glaze and grill until golden. Use a spatula to gently lift the soufflés onto serving plates and serve immediately, with the salad.

This dish was made up out of the massive smashed-up pumpkins the contestants left at Highgrove after The Great British Village Show final. Some of these whoppers needed six Army lads to lift them off the trucks.

ROAST PUMPKIN AND PARMESAN SOUFFLÉ

serves 4

½ medium pumpkin or
   butternut squash
olive oil
salt and pepper
25g (scant 1oz) unsalted butter
   plus extra for greasing
25g (scant 1oz) plain flour
150ml (5fl oz) milk
25g (scant 1oz) Parmesan,
   finely grated
2 fresh sage leaves,
   finely chopped
3 eggs, separated

tip   Instead of pumpkin or butternut
squash, you can use other varieties of
winter squash.

1 Preheat the oven to 180°C fan (200°C/gas 6). Grease four ramekins with butter, and set aside.

2 Peel the pumpkin, remove the seeds and central fibres, and cut the flesh into cubes. Place the cubes in a roasting tin, drizzle with olive oil, and season with salt and pepper. Roast for 40–45 minutes until tender and caramelized. Remove from the oven and blend in a food processor to a rough purée. You need 150g (5½oz) purée for the soufflés. Set aside to cool.

3 Meanwhile, melt the butter in a large saucepan over a medium heat. Add the flour and mix well. Cook over a low heat for 2–3 minutes, stirring with a wooden spoon. Gradually add the milk, stirring constantly to prevent any lumps from forming. When all the milk has been added, reduce the heat to very low and cook for a further 5–6 minutes.

4 Remove from the heat and season to taste, then set aside to cool slightly. Stir the roasted pumpkin purée, Parmesan, and sage into the warm mixture. Set aside to cool further before beating in the egg yolks.

5 In a clean, dry bowl, whisk the egg whites until they hold medium peaks. Use a metal spoon to fold the egg whites into the soufflé mixture, to combine. Divide the mixture among the soufflé dishes and smooth the top using a palette knife. Bake for 15–20 minutes until well risen and evenly coloured. Remove from the oven and serve immediately.

I think the best place to buy pork is either at farmers' markets or butchers, particularly if you want to find a cut like shoulder. Minced shoulder is juicy and full of flavour, so is ideal for terrines and pâtés, which can sometimes be quite dry.

PORK AND CHICKEN LIVER TERRINE

serves 10–12

24 slices of streaky bacon
250g (9oz) minced shoulder
  of pork
250g (9oz) minced chicken
375ml (13fl oz) double cream
3 tbsp chopped fresh parsley
3 tbsp chopped fresh chives
2 tbsp chopped fresh tarragon
1 egg
100ml (3½fl oz) Armagnac or
  other brandy
2 shallots, chopped
salt and pepper
400g (14oz) chicken livers
200g (7oz) sliced cooked ham

to serve
chutney
dressed mixed salad leaves

1 Preheat the oven to 200°C fan (220°C/gas 7).

2 Use the bacon to line the bottom and sides of a terrine mould measuring 28 x 9 x 9cm (11 x 3½ x 3½in), making sure you leave enough overhang so the bacon will cover the top of the terrine mixture.

3 Put the minced meats into a large bowl and work in the cream, herbs, and egg with a wooden spatula. Stir in the Armagnac and shallots. Season with 1 tsp salt and some pepper. Set aside.

4 In a hot frying pan, sauté the chicken livers for 1–2 minutes to brown all sides. Remove to a plate and allow to cool.

5 Place some of the minced mixture on the bottom of the terrine mould. Layer up the chicken livers, ham, and the rest of the mince mixture, pressing well as you go. When the mould is full to the top, fold over the bacon. Cover with the lid or a piece of foil. Place the mould in a roasting tin of hot water and cook in the oven for 1 hour.

6 Remove from the oven and allow to cool completely. Cover the mould with fresh foil and refrigerate overnight. Turn out the terrine and slice, then serve with chutney and salad.

Potted meats and fish have been around since the end of the sixteenth century. This method of preserving food became very fashionable amongst the rich at their grand country houses. I've used both duck and pork here, but if you prefer you can use just one or the other.

POTTED DUCK AND PORK

serves 4

confit
4 duck legs, about 250g (9oz)
   each
300g (11oz) lean pork, diced
115g (4oz) sea salt
1kg (2¼lb) duck fat or lard
salt and pepper

to garnish
1 tbsp balsamic vinegar
1 tbsp extra virgin olive oil
50g (1¾oz) mixed salad leaves

to serve
toasted brioche or Melba toast
tomato and apple chutney
   (see page 196)

1 For the confit, dust the duck legs and pork separately with the sea salt, cover, and leave for 8–10 hours in a cool place.

2 Preheat the oven to 180°C fan (200°C/gas 6).

3 Rinse the salt off the duck legs and pork with cold water. Dry with kitchen paper. Melt half of the duck fat in a heavy-bottomed ovenproof pan and submerge the duck legs in the fat. Do the same with the pork in another pan. Cover both pans, place in the oven, and cook for 2–2½ hours until the meat is tender and you can twist out the duck thigh bone easily).

4 Remove the duck legs and pork from the fat and leave both fat and meat to cool. Once the fat is tepid, strain it through a fine sieve into a clean saucepan, bring up to the boil, and skim. Cool again, then strain once more. Put the duck legs and pork in a clean container, cover with the fat (ensuring there are no air holes), cover, and refrigerate for up to 3 days.

5 Shred the pork and the meat from the duck legs into a bowl, discarding any duck skin. Add the fat and season with salt and pepper. Line a mould (either a terrine or ramekins) with cling film. Spoon in the duck and pork mixture and press down well. Cover with more cling film, then place in the fridge to set.

6 If set in a terrine mould, cut the potted meat into thick slices. Whisk the balsamic vinegar, oil, and seasoning together, and use to dress the salad leaves. Serve the potted meat with the salad, toasted brioche, and chutney.

Garlic bread tastes good, but with cheese it tastes even better. I use Brie as it goes all runny when cooked, but any cheese will do as long as it melts well.

FAB CHEESY GARLIC BREAD

serves 4–6

1 whole garlic bulb,
   cloves peeled
1–2 tsp chopped fresh
   flat-leaf parsley
juice of 1 lemon
75g (2½oz) soft butter
salt and pepper
115g (4oz) Brie cheese, diced
1 medium baguette

1 Preheat the oven to 200°C fan (220°C/gas 7).

2 Finely chop the garlic in a blender. Add the parsley and lemon juice and blend briefly. Add the soft butter and seasoning, and then the diced Brie. Blend until smooth.

3 Cut the baguette into thick slices without cutting all the way through the base. Spread both sides of each slice with the garlic butter, pushing it right down into the cuts.

4 Wrap the baguette in foil, then bake for 10–15 minutes until crisp and golden. Serve hot.

A rarebit is not just cheese on toast, and there are many twists on the classic Welsh rarebit. The one here is topped with smoked bacon. Scotch rarebit has a fried egg on it, and if Welsh rarebit is topped with gherkins and onions it becomes Irish rarebit.

YORKSHIRE RAREBIT

serves 4–6

4–6 thin slices of white bread
knob of butter, for spreading
12–18 slices good smoked
   streaky bacon

rarebit
375g (13oz) strong Cheddar
   cheese, grated
3½ tbsp milk
3½ tbsp double cream
1 egg, beaten
1 egg yolk
½ tbsp mustard powder
25g (scant 1oz) fresh white
   breadcrumbs
30g (1oz) plain flour
dash of Worcestershire sauce
dash of Tabasco sauce
salt and pepper

1 Preheat the grill to high.

2 To make the rarebit, put the cheese, milk, and cream in a heavy saucepan and gently warm until the cheese has melted, stirring frequently. Take care not to let the mixture boil. Remove from the heat and cool slightly.

3 Add the egg, egg yolk, mustard, breadcrumbs, flour, and Worcestershire and Tabasco sauces. Season and set aside.

4 Toast the bread on one side under the grill. Place in a flameproof dish, arranging the slices untoasted sides up and side by side. Butter lightly. Grill the bacon until crisp, then arrange on top of the bread.

5 Pour the rarebit mixture over the bacon and bread, making sure you spread it to the edges. Grill until bubbling and speckled with brown.

6 Remove from the grill and cool a bit before serving with tomato and apple chutney (see page 196).

tip   If you prefer, you can use a chunky farmhouse bread instead. Before spreading the rarebit over the bacon, you may need to firm it up in the fridge, so it stays in place.

I was brought up on a farm that backed onto a field full of peas. My mother and I used to spend ages picking and eating them when we'd take the dogs for a walk. It was like going to a great pick-your-own fruit farm.

SALMON, CHERRY TOMATO, AND PEA FRITTATA

serves 6–8

1–2 tbsp olive oil
1 bunch of spring onions, sliced
1 garlic clove, crushed
175g (6oz) cherry tomatoes, halved
6 eggs
small bunch of fresh mint, chopped (optional)
sea salt and crushed black pepper
200g (7oz) cooked salmon fillet, skinned and flaked
125g (4½oz) frozen peas, thawed and drained
extra virgin olive oil

1 Preheat the grill.

2 Heat the olive oil in a medium non-stick frying pan that can be placed under the grill. Fry the spring onions and garlic for a few minutes to soften before adding the tomatoes.

3 Lightly beat the eggs with the mint and season with salt and pepper. Swirl the egg mixture into the pan, then scatter over the flaked salmon and the peas. Cook over a medium heat for 3–4 minutes until almost set.

4 Drizzle with extra virgin olive oil, then transfer to the grill and cook for 2–3 minutes until lightly browned and cooked through. Serve warm or cold, cut into wedges.

Everybody loves a quiche, and at village shows all over the country you will find stalls selling many different flavours. This classic is the one for me. If you don't want to make your own pastry, you can use readymade.

BACON, CHEESE, AND TOMATO QUICHE

serves 4

pastry
200g (7oz) plain flour, plus
   extra for dusting
pinch of salt
100g (3½oz) butter, plus extra
   for greasing

filling
200g (7oz) smoked back or
   streaky bacon, chopped
250g (9oz) Cheddar cheese,
   grated
3 tomatoes, sliced
5 eggs, beaten
100ml (3½fl oz) milk
200ml (7fl oz) double cream
salt and pepper
2 sprigs of fresh thyme,
   stalks discarded

tip If you don't have baking beans, you can use flour or uncooked rice to fill the parchment-lined pastry case.

illustrated on pages 52–53

1 To make the pastry, sift the flour and salt into a large bowl. Rub in the butter until you have a soft breadcrumb texture. Add enough cold water (about 2 tbsp) to form a firm dough. Wrap in cling film and leave to rest in the fridge for 30 minutes.

2 Roll out the pastry on a lightly floured surface and use to line a well-buttered 22cm (8½in) flan dish. Don't cut off the excess pastry yet. Chill again for 30 minutes.

3 Preheat the oven to 190°C fan (210°C/gas 6½).

4 Line the bottom of the pastry case with baking parchment or foil, then fill it with baking beans. Place on a baking tray and bake blind for 15–20 minutes. Remove the baking beans and parchment or foil, and return to the oven to bake for a further 5 minutes. Set aside.

5 Reduce the oven temperature to 160°C fan (180°C/gas 4).

6 Fry the bacon pieces until crisp, then drain on kitchen paper. Sprinkle the cheese over the pastry base. Arrange the sliced tomatoes on the cheese and scatter the bacon on top.

7 Combine the eggs, milk, and cream in a bowl and season well. Pour over the bacon and cheese. Sprinkle the thyme leaves over the surface. Bake for 40–45 minutes until the filling is just set. Remove from the oven and allow to cool.

8 Before serving, trim off the excess pastry to get a perfect edge, then cut the quiche into wedges.

A bridie is a savoury flat pie made from shortcrust pastry. I tried one when I was in Scotland watching a football match — it was very welcome at half-time as the day was very cold.

BRIDIES

makes 4 pies

2 onions, sliced
1 garlic clove, crushed
knob of butter
olive oil for frying
115g (4oz) mushrooms, sliced
1 glass red wine
dash of balsamic vinegar
225g (8oz) lean beef, minced
few sprigs of fresh thyme
salt and pepper
500g (1lb 2oz) readymade
   shortcrust pastry
1 egg, beaten with 1 egg yolk

1 Preheat the oven to 200°C fan (220°C/gas 7).

2 Sauté the onions and garlic in the butter and a splash of olive oil until caramelized. Add the mushrooms, wine, and balsamic vinegar. Reduce down for a few minutes, then remove from the heat and allow to cool.

3 Mix together the minced beef, thyme, and seasoning.

4 Roll out the pastry to about 5mm (¼in) thick and cut out four large oval shapes like rugby balls. Each should be about the size of a small side plate. Take a handful of the beef mix (about one-quarter) and place on one half of each pastry oval. Flatten the beef, keeping it clear of the edges, then spread over the onion mix. Fold the other half of the pastry oval over the filling to form a pasty shape. Seal the edges well and brush the top of each bridie with the egg wash.

5 Place on a baking tray and bake for 15–20 minutes until the pastry is nicely browned. These are best eaten hot, although they can also be served cold.

When I was a kid I seemed to live on croquettes, as well as cold lamb and mint sauce. This is a kind of grown-up version. You can make these with pumpkin or butternut squash, both of which are around all year.

ROAST PUMPKIN AND POLENTA CROQUETTES

makes 6 croquettes

1 small pumpkin
4 tbsp olive oil, plus extra
    for drizzling
salt and pepper
2 spring onions, finely chopped
2 garlic cloves, crushed
150g (5½oz) mashed potato
1 egg yolk
2–3 tbsp chopped fresh
    coriander leaves

coating
75g (2½oz) plain flour
2 eggs, beaten
100g (3½oz) "instant"
    polenta flour

1 Preheat the oven to 200°C fan (220°C/gas 7).

2 Peel the pumpkin, remove the seeds and central fibres, and cut the flesh into wedges. Place the wedges in a roasting tin, drizzle with olive oil, and season with salt and pepper. Roast for 45–50 minutes until tender.

3 Transfer the wedges to a food processor and blend to make a rough purée. You need 250g (9oz) purée for the croquettes. Transfer to a bowl and allow to cool slightly.

4 Add the spring onions, garlic, mashed potato, and egg yolk to the pumpkin and mix well to combine. Stir in the coriander and season with salt and pepper. Divide the mixture into six and form each portion into a log shape.

5 Dip the croquettes in the flour to coat all over, then in the beaten egg, and finally in the polenta, pressing it on and shaking off any excess.

6 Heat the 4 tbsp oil in a non-stick frying pan and fry the croquettes for 3–4 minutes on each side until golden brown and crisp, turning to cook and colour all sides. Serve hot.

tip   If more convenient, you can chill the croquettes once they are shaped and coated, until you are ready to fry them.

I made this first with tomatoes from my garden and the flavour was amazing. It isn't anywhere near the same if you use supermarket tomatoes. Speaking of those, I couldn't believe my eyes when I saw a label that said "grown for flavour". What else is a tomato grown for?

TOMATO AND BASIL SORBET

makes about 1 litre (1¾ pints)

12 large ripe tomatoes
¼ tsp sea salt
250g (9oz) caster sugar
4 tbsp liquid glucose
25g (scant 1oz) fresh
   basil leaves
vodka to serve (optional)

1 Purée the tomatoes with the salt in a food processor or blender, then rub through a sieve into a bowl. Chill.

2 Combine the sugar, glucose, and 200ml (7fl oz) water in a heavy saucepan and heat gently until the sugar has dissolved and the syrup is clear. Bring to the boil and boil for a couple of minutes. Take off the heat, add the basil, and leave to steep in the hot syrup as it cools. Strain the syrup and chill.

3 When ready to freeze, combine the puréed tomatoes and basil-infused syrup. Churn in an ice cream machine until almost firm, then transfer to a suitable container, seal, and pop into the freezer to finish freezing.

4 Serve scooped into glasses, on its own or with a splash of vodka added to each glass.

Steve Rutterford was the winner of the heaviest leek category at The Great British Village Show at Petworth House and this is a favourite recipe of his. He says, "The tea takes the sweetness off the tomatoes and gives them a nice tang. Serve these as part of your breakfast".

STEVE RUTTERFORD'S TOMATOES IN TEA

1 Take some soft ripe tomatoes and cut them in half. Put them in a pan with a little bit of oil and fry them until they start to go dark and soft (not burnt).

2 Pour in ½ cup of mashed (stewed) cold tea – left over from the pot the night before. (Strain if you used tea leaves.) Add some salt and pepper. Reduce to thicken, and serve hot.

2

main courses

Pork and Runner Bean Stir-Fry **Roast Belly of Pork with Root Vegetables**
Spare Ribs with BBQ Sauce **Sausages with White Bean Mash and**
Tomato Veal and Ham Raised Pie **Hand Pies** Braised Lamb Shank Pie
Pan-Fried Fillet of Beef with Fat Chips and Slow-Roasted Tomatoes
Rump of Lamb with Little Gem and Buttered Peas **Lemony Leg of Lamb**
Roast New Potatoes with Grain Mustard and Rack of Lamb **Lamb Chops**
with Stewed Beans and Rosemary Lamb-Stuffed Aubergines **Sherie**
Plumb's Lasagne S.A.S.S.F (Sherie's After-Show Stir-Fry) **Roast Poussin**
with Risotto and Grapes Chicken, Leek, and Tarragon Pie **Breast of**
Chicken with Pancetta and Creamed Leeks Savoy Cabbage with Roast
Duck Breast **Honeyed Duck with Chicory** Sautéed Courgettes with
Sesame and Soy Sauce, and Duck Confit **Escalopes of Salmon with Sorrel**
Sauce Stuffed Sea Bass with Onions, Herbs, and Honey **Pan-Fried Halibut**
with Glazed Carrots Seared Tuna Steaks with Grape and Dandelion Salad
Pickled French Beans with Pan-Fried Red Mullet Fillets Mackerel
Parcels with Celery and Pancetta **Fish Cakes and Pickled Cucumber**
Pan-Fried Salmon with Tomato and Herb Sauce **Jerusalem Artichoke**
and Clam Risotto Jan Kisiel's Courgette Bake **Clive Bevan's Leek Pie**
Cauliflower Risotto **Potato and Haricot Mash with Truffle Oil** Potato
Gnocchi **Béarnaise Sauce** Red Wine Sauce

At the shows I saw some of the best runner beans ever. Fresh runner beans should be able to be snapped in half and not be stringy, which you often find happens with the supermarket ones.

PORK AND RUNNER BEAN STIR-FRY

serves 4

2 tbsp olive oil
400g (14oz) pork fillet
  (tenderloin), cut into
  thin strips
5 shallots, sliced
4 garlic cloves, crushed
2 yellow peppers, deseeded
  and thinly sliced
2 red peppers, deseeded and
  thinly sliced
400g (14oz) runner beans,
  shredded
2.5cm (1in) piece fresh ginger,
  peeled and cut into strips
4 tbsp soy sauce
4 tbsp honey
2 tbsp toasted sesame oil
170g (6oz) hoisin sauce
grated zest and juice of 2 limes
300g (10½oz) pak choi,
  shredded
4 tsp sesame seeds, toasted

1 Heat 1 tbsp of the oil in a large non-stick frying pan or wok and brown the meat all over until nicely coloured. Remove from the pan and set aside.

2 Heat the remaining oil in the pan and sauté the shallots and garlic for a few minutes, to soften. Add the yellow and red peppers, runner beans, and ginger, and stir-fry for 5–6 minutes.

3 Mix the soy sauce, honey, sesame oil, and hoisin sauce together in a bowl. Add to the pan together with the lime zest and juice, pak choi, and pork slices. Stir-fry for 4–5 minutes until the vegetables are tender.

4 Serve hot, sprinkled with the toasted sesame seeds. Rice noodles or steamed rice are good accompaniments.

The runner beans had a maximum points value of 18, which was broken down into five categories:
Condition 5 points
Uniformity 4 points
Shape 3 points
Size 3 points
Colour 3 points

Entrants had to present six beans for the judges's scrutiny. Unlike in the world of giant vegetables, where size is everything, the key to success in this class is uniformity.

THE RUNNER BEAN CLASS

Head Judge Medwyn Williams

"Judges are looking for long, straight, uniform, fresh, firm pods which snap readily, are of good colour, and have no outward signs of the seeds in the pods."

Judge John Trim

"To test runner beans for freshness, snap a bean in half. If there is a string holding the two halves together, the bean will be tough. To test for freshness in the supermarket, press the bean between finger and thumb where the seed pods form. If you hear a pop, the bean is fresh."

Judge Gerald Treweek

"Runner beans are best grown in a deeply dug trench with loads of manure. This is done in the winter months. Top the trench up with soil and add plenty of ground limestone. Beans need a pH of 6.5–7. Do not apply feed at this stage. Set the beans in pots in the greenhouse in May and plant out when the plants are large enough. When flowers start to set, apply high nitrogen soluble feed every week."

David Miles at The Great British Village Show at Montacute House

Belly is the best piece of meat on a pig, and that's saying something when you can eat everything but the squeak. It's worth seeking out suppliers of meat from rare breed pigs because it tastes far better than the pork some supermarkets sell.

ROAST BELLY OF PORK WITH ROOT VEGETABLES

serves 4

pork
1 belly of pork joint, skin on, about 1.8kg (4lb), skin scored
4 tbsp cider vinegar
2 tbsp pork dripping or butter
8 bay leaves, crushed
8 garlic cloves, finely chopped
2 tbsp sea salt
1 tbsp black peppercorns, crushed
red wine sauce (see page 117), to serve

vegetables
400g (14oz) carrots, peeled and cut into long wedges
6 shallots, peeled
4 parsnips, peeled and cut into long wedges
1 whole garlic bulb, sliced crossways in half
3 sprigs of fresh thyme
1 tbsp olive oil
250g (9oz) spinach leaves

1 The night before, pour boiling water over the pork skin, then rub the joint with the cider vinegar. Place the joint on a plate in the fridge, uncovered, and leave overnight.

2 Preheat the oven to 200°C fan (220°C/gas 7). Spread the dripping, crushed bay leaves, garlic, salt, and pepper all over the pork. Set aside for 30 minutes so the flavours can develop.

3 Place the pork skin side up on a wire rack set over an empty roasting tin. Roast for 1 hour, then remove from the oven and reduce the oven temperature to 180°C fan (200°C/gas 6).

4 Spread the prepared vegetables in another roasting tin and add the thyme, olive oil, and a wineglass of water. Lift the pork on its rack off the empty roasting tin and pour any fat that has gathered in the tin over the vegetables. Set the pork on its rack over the tin of vegetables and place in the oven. Roast for a further hour, basting the pork and vegetables from time to time with the juices. The crackling should be crisp and golden.

5 Remove the pork from the wire rack and allow to rest in a warm place for 15 minutes. Meanwhile, toss the spinach leaves with the hot vegetables. Remove from the tin, draining off any fat, and keep warm in a serving dish.

6 Remove the crackling in one piece and portion it, then carve the pork. Serve with the root vegetables and red wine sauce.

There are some great suppliers of pork popping up at farmers' markets all over the UK. Martin Martindale at Winchester's farmers' market is one of the best. I love spare ribs, and these are particularly delicious. Try them with a Caesar salad.

SPARE RIBS WITH BBQ SAUCE

serves 4

1.8kg (4lb) pork spare ribs
2 medium onions, finely
   chopped or sliced
4 garlic cloves, crushed
olive oil for frying
2 red chillies, finely chopped
2 tsp fennel seeds, crushed
115g (4oz) dark brown sugar
100ml (3½fl oz) dark soy sauce
600ml (1 pint) tomato ketchup,
   home-made (see page 205)
   or bought
salt and pepper

1 Preheat the oven to 180°C fan (200°C/gas 6). Place the spare ribs side by side in a roasting tin and roast for 20–25 minutes.

2 While they are cooking, fry the onions and garlic in a little olive oil with the chillies, fennel seeds, and sugar. When the onions are soft, stir in the soy sauce and ketchup and season with salt and pepper. Bring to the boil and simmer for a few minutes to combine all the flavours. Leave to one side to cool.

3 Remove the ribs from the oven and brush liberally with the sauce, using about half of it. Return to the oven and roast for a further 10 minutes to glaze the ribs. Serve hot, with the rest of the sauce in a jug.

G Scott butchers in York is where I always go when I'm up north in Yorkshire — it's where I used to queue up with my gran for a slice of York ham. They not only produce great pork and sausages (available online, by the way), but fab beef from rare and traditional breeds.

SAUSAGES WITH WHITE BEAN MASH AND TOMATO

serves 4

vegetable oil
8 meaty sausages
red wine sauce (see page 117), heated to serve

tomato confit
1.5kg (3lb 3oz) ripe, large, meaty tomatoes
4 tbsp olive oil
1 medium onion, very finely sliced
10 garlic cloves, coarsely chopped
10 small, fresh basil leaves, shredded
salt

white bean mash
700g (1½lb) Maris Piper potatoes, peeled and quartered
salt and black pepper
450g (1lb) cooked or canned haricot or cannellini beans
80g (scant 3oz) butter, softened
125ml (4fl oz) double cream
pinch of freshly grated nutmeg

1 First, prepare the tomato confit. Peel and deseed the tomatoes (see page 14), then coarsely chop the tomato flesh. Heat the oil in a pan and fry the onion for 5 minutes. Add the garlic and fry for a further minute. Add the tomatoes and bring to the boil, then reduce the heat and simmer gently for 30–40 minutes until soft and well reduced. Halfway through, stir in the shredded basil. Season with salt, then purée briefly in a blender. The confit should be thick and not a pouring sauce. Set aside until ready to serve.

2 For the mash, put the potatoes in a pan and cover with water. Add a good pinch of salt and bring to the boil. Cook for 20–25 minutes until tender.

3 Meanwhile, heat a little oil in a non-stick frying pan over a low to medium heat and cook the sausages for 20–25 minutes, turning frequently, until golden brown and cooked through.

4 Drain the potatoes and return to the pan. Stir in the beans to break up the potatoes, then beat in the butter and cream a little at a time. Pass though a potato ricer or sieve to remove the bean skins. Season with salt, pepper, and nutmeg.

5 Spoon the mash onto warmed plates, add the sausages, and top with the tomato confit. Drizzle the red wine sauce around.

tip   Any left over tomato confit can be stored in the fridge for a few days, although it is best if eaten when freshly made.

The French and Italians eat a lot of veal, but in the UK it has fallen out of favour because of the way veal calves were traditionally kept. However, a few UK producers are farming organic free-range veal that is rosy in colour. You can also use chicken for this pie.

VEAL AND HAM RAISED PIE

serves 8

hot water crust pastry
450g (1lb) plain flour
½ tsp salt
1 tbsp icing sugar
1 egg, beaten
80g (scant 3oz) butter
80g (scant 3oz) lard
1 egg, beaten, for glaze

filling
450g (1lb) stewing veal,
    chopped coarsely into 5mm
    (¼in) pieces
450g (1lb) cooked ham,
    chopped coarsely into 5mm
    (¼in) pieces
4 tbsp chopped fresh
    flat-leaf parsley
grated zest and juice of
    1 small lemon
pepper
4 hard-boiled eggs, peeled
200ml (7fl oz) jellied stock,
    home-made or bought

1 Preheat the oven to 200°C fan (220°C/gas 7). Place a heavy baking tray in the oven.

2 To make the pastry, mix the flour, salt, and icing sugar in a large bowl. Make a dip in the middle, pour the egg into it, and toss a liberal covering of flour over the egg. Put 200ml (7fl oz) water, the butter, and lard into a saucepan and bring slowly to the boil to melt the fat. Once the liquid is boiling, pour it onto the flour and egg, mixing with a knife. Knead until all the egg streaks have gone and the pastry is smooth. Use immediately to make your pie, because as the pastry cools it will harden and will then be unworkable.

3 Cut off one-third of the pastry and set this aside for the lid. Roll out the larger piece to an oblong shape large enough to line the bottom and sides of a hinged 26 x 13.5 x 7cm (10½ x 5½ x 3in) tin, with an overhang of about 2cm (¾in). Use the pastry to line the tin. Roll out the remaining pastry to fit the top of the pie and set aside.

4 Combine the veal and ham in a bowl and mix in the parsley, lemon zest and juice, and plenty of pepper (you won't need salt as the ham will be quite salty). Spread a layer of about half of the meat mixture in the pastry-lined tin. Arrange the eggs lengthwise in a line down the centre. Cover the eggs with the rest of the meat, pressing down gently.

5 Brush the edges of the pastry case with a little beaten egg. Place the pastry lid on top of the filling, and pinch and crimp the edges of the case and lid to seal, trimming away any excess pastry. Use the pastry trimmings to make decorative leaves. Brush the top of the pie with beaten egg and make a hole in the centre. Arrange the pastry leaves on top and brush them with the egg glaze. Set the pie on the baking tray in the oven and cook for 40–45 minutes until golden brown.

6 Remove the pie from the oven and leave it to cool for about 10 minutes. Heat the jellied stock until it is liquid, then pour it very slowly through a small funnel into the hole in the pie lid. Leave the pie to cool, then refrigerate for up to 2 hours before cutting into slices to serve.

tip Trim the white from the top and bottom of each hard–boiled egg so that they fit neatly "back to back" and so that each slice of pie will include egg yolk.

I learnt the art of making these at Melton Mowbray, which is of course famous for its pork pie. Savoury pies used to be made for people to take with them on hunts. They would throw away the case and only eat the filling. I wonder what the case was made of.

HAND PIES

makes 8 pies

pastry
500g (1lb) plain flour
250g (8oz) butter, diced
salt and pepper
1 egg, beaten
1 egg, beaten, for glaze

filling
2 tbsp sunflower oil
1kg (2¼lb) braising beef, cut into very large chunks
4 carrots, peeled and cut into very large chunks
1 large onion, roughly chopped
1 garlic clove, chopped
small pinch of chilli flakes
4 tbsp plain flour
big splash of basamic vinegar
1 bottle full-bodied red wine
1 bouquet garni (small bunch of parsley stalks, few bay leaves, and small bunch of thyme tied together with string)
150g (5½oz) Stilton cheese, crumbled

1 To make the pastry, tip the flour, butter, a pinch of salt, and some pepper into a food processor and pulse until the mixture has the texture of breadcrumbs. Pour in the egg and 70–100ml (3–3½fl oz) water, and pulse again until the pastry comes together. Wrap and chill in the fridge for at least 30 minutes before using.

2 Preheat the oven to 160°C fan (180°C/gas 4).

3 Heat the sunflower oil in a large flameproof casserole dish until smoking. Add half the beef and leave it to brown for about 5 minutes (don't be tempted to prod, stir, or lift it up). Stir once, then continue to brown the meat. Remove it to a plate using a slotted spoon. Repeat with the second batch of beef.

4 Once the second batch of beef has been removed from the casserole, add the carrots, onion, garlic, and chilli flakes to the pan and cook for 8–10 minutes until the vegetables are starting to soften. Stir in the flour and cook for 2 minutes until the flour begins to brown. Add the vinegar and allow the mixture to simmer for 2 minutes, then stir in the red wine.

5 Tip the beef and any juices back into the casserole and season generously with salt and a little pepper. Bring to the boil, then add the bouquet garni. Cover and place in the oven to cook for about 2 hours until the meat is meltingly tender. Remove from the oven and leave to cool.

6 Turn the oven up to 220°C fan (240°C/gas 9) and put a baking tray in to heat.

7 Roll out the pastry on a floured surface to 3mm (⅛in) thick and cut out pieces to line eight individual pie tins or foil trays. Spoon the cooled filling into the pastry cases and sprinkle on the Stilton. Cut lids for the pies from the remaining pastry. Wet the pastry edges with a little water and place the lids on top. Seal the edges by pressing together, then trim away any excess pastry. Brush the tops of the pies with egg to glaze.

8 Place the pies on the hot tray and bake for 10 minutes, then lower the oven temperature to 180°C fan (200°C/gas 6) and bake for a further 30–35 minutes until the tops are golden. Remove from the oven and leave to rest for 10 minutes. The pies should now turn out of their tins easily and the pastry bases should be crisp. The pies are best eaten hot, but can also be served cold.

Lamb shanks used to be given away for pence when I was cheffing in London in the early 90s, but now they're trendy and everybody's cooking them. The best way to cook shanks is for a long time so that the meat becomes so tender it breaks down.

BRAISED LAMB SHANK PIE

serves 6–8

filling
50g (1¾oz) plain flour
salt and pepper
6 lamb shanks
2 tbsp olive oil
4 red onions, quartered
8 garlic cloves, peeled
1 bottle full-bodied red wine
300ml (10fl oz) beef stock
2 tbsp finely chopped
    fresh rosemary
3 tbsp redcurrant jelly

pastry
400g (14oz) readymade
    puff pastry
beaten egg to glaze

1 Season the flour with a good pinch of salt and plenty of pepper. Dust the shanks. Heat the oil in a large, heavy pan or flameproof casserole dish and brown the shanks all over.

2 Add any remaining flour, the onions, and garlic and stir well. Pour in the wine and stock, and add the rosemary, redcurrant jelly, and a good grinding of black pepper. Bring to the boil, then cover and turn down the heat to a very gentle simmer. Cook for about 2 hours until the meat is falling off the bone and the sauce is rich and thick.

3 Preheat the oven to 200°C fan (220°C/gas 7).

4 Remove the shank bones from the pan and reserve three of them. Flake the meat into small pieces in the pan. Fill a 2 litre (3½ pint) pie dish with the lamb filling.

5 Roll out the pastry to about 3mm (⅛in) thick and to a shape about 2.5cm (1in) larger than the dish. Cut a 2cm (¾in) strip from around the pastry shape. Brush the rim of the dish with a little water and place the pastry strip on the rim, pressing it down. Sit the three reserved lamb bones in the pie filling at intervals along the length of the dish, to act as pie funnels.

6 Cut three slits in the pastry lid in the same position as the lamb bones. Place the lid over the dish and slide the slits down over the bones. Press the edges of the pastry lid to the strip on the rim to seal. Trim off any excess pastry and crimp the edges. Brush with beaten egg. Bake for 30–35 minutes until the pastry is crisp and golden. Serve hot.

Everyone loves steak and chips – but with big chips, not pommes frites, and with juicy tomatoes. Slow-roasting is a great way of using good tomatoes because it really concentrates their flavour. Instead of basil oil, you can serve the steaks with béarnaise sauce (see page 116).

PAN-FRIED FILLET OF BEEF WITH FAT CHIPS AND SLOW-ROASTED TOMATOES

serves 4

6 plum or vine tomatoes, cut
  in half
salt and pepper
2 tbsp chopped fresh thyme
2 tbsp extra virgin olive oil plus
  extra for drizzling
4 fillet steaks, about 225g
  (8oz) each
30g (1oz) unsalted butter
4 large potatoes, peeled and
  cut into fat chips
vegetable oil, for deep-frying
4 tsp fresh basil oil (see below)

1 Preheat the oven to 120°C fan (140°C/gas 1).

2 Place the tomatoes cut side up on a baking tray, season with salt and pepper, and sprinkle with the fresh thyme. Drizzle over some olive oil. Slow-roast for 45 minutes to 1 hour.

3 Season the steaks. Heat a heavy frying pan or griddle. When hot, place the steaks in the dry pan and colour well on one side. Turn the steaks over and add the butter and 2 tbsp olive oil. Cooking times from now on are 3–4 minutes each side for rare; 5 minutes each side for medium; and 6–7 minutes each side for well done.

4 Deep-fry the chips in hot oil for a few minutes, without colouring. Remove and allow to rest for a few minutes, then plunge again into the hot oil and fry for 8–10 minutes until golden and cooked. Remove and drain on kitchen paper. Season with salt.

5 Pile some chips on each warmed plate and add a steak. Place the roasted tomatoes alongside and drizzle with a little basil oil. Serve immediately.

tip To make basil oil, blitz a bunch of fresh basil in a mini food processor with salt and pepper, then gradually blend in 125–150ml (4–5fl oz) olive oil. Strain if you like. The oil can be kept in a bottle in the fridge for 2–3 days.

illustrated on pages 76–77

Rump of lamb has been a feature on modern British chefs' menus for some years now. Ask your butcher for lamb rumps or chumps and get him to bone them out. You may have to order them, but they're worth the wait.

RUMP OF LAMB WITH LITTLE GEM AND BUTTERED PEAS

serves 4

lamb
2 tbsp vegetable oil, plus extra
  for frying
40–50g (1½–1¾oz) fresh
  rosemary leaves, chopped
2 garlic cloves, crushed
15g (½oz) black peppercorns,
  crushed
4 rumps of lamb, about 250g
  (9oz) each

little gem and peas
400g (14oz) freshly shelled peas
8 button onions, peeled, or
  8 shallots, peeled and cut
  in half
100g (3½oz) butter
1 tsp salt
1½ tbsp sugar
1 bouquet garni
2 Little Gem lettuces, cored
  and finely sliced
pepper

1 Preheat the oven to 190°C fan (210°C/gas 6½).

2 Put the oil, rosemary, garlic, and peppercorns into a bowl and add the lamb. Make sure everything is thoroughly mixed together (adding a little extra oil if necessary), then set aside to marinate for up to 1 hour.

3 Heat a thick-bottomed, ovenproof pan. When it starts to smoke, add a little vegetable oil, then colour the lamb all over, fat side down first. Transfer the pan to the oven and cook for about 8 minutes (or 12–15 minutes for well done). Remove from the oven and leave to rest for 5 minutes.

4 While the lamb is cooking, combine the peas, onions, butter, salt, sugar, and bouquet garni in a heavy saucepan. Cover tightly and place on a low heat. Cook gently for 10 minutes. Discard the bouquet garni. Season with pepper to taste, then add the lettuce. Replace the lid and remove from the heat. Keep warm until the lamb is ready.

5 To serve, slice the lamb and arrange on top of the peas.

I had a look at a British food website and was shocked to see that they said New Zealand lamb is the best. What a load of rubbish. Here in the UK we produce the finest meat in the world and we should be proud of it too. So stop buying that other stuff and stick with what's best.

LEMONY LEG OF LAMB

serves 4

1 leg of lamb, about 1.5kg (3lb 3oz)
salt and pepper
grated zest and juice of 3 lemons
3 garlic cloves, chopped
3 sprigs of fresh rosemary, leaves chopped
100ml (3½fl oz) olive oil
100g (3½oz) piece of fresh ginger, peeled and grated
1 onion, roughly chopped
1 leek, roughly chopped
2 lemongrass sticks, bashed

1 Preheat the oven to 180°C fan (200°C/gas 6). Lightly score the lamb and season with salt and pepper.

2 Mix together the lemon zest and juice with the garlic, rosemary, and olive oil, then add the grated ginger.

3 Put the onion, leek, and lemongrass in a roasting tin and place the leg of lamb on top. Rub the lemon mixture all over the lamb. Cover with greaseproof paper and then with foil. Roast the lamb, allowing 40 minutes to each 1kg (2¼lb) plus an extra 20 minutes.

4 When the lamb has been roasting for 70 minutes, remove the foil and greaseproof and baste with the juices in the tin. Put back into the oven to brown, basting from time to time.

5 When cooked, allow to stand for 5 minutes before carving. Serve with boiled new potatoes tossed with lots of butter.

tip Place the squeezed lemons in the roasting tin under the lamb. This will improve and intensify the lemony flavour of the dish. If you like, use the vegetables and juices in the roasting tin to make a delicious gravy.

I call this chef's food — simple, no-nonsense, full of flavour lamb with freshly cooked new potatoes and mustard. What could be better?

ROAST NEW POTATOES WITH GRAIN MUSTARD AND RACK OF LAMB

serves 2

450g (1lb) new potatoes
2 sprigs of fresh thyme
salt and pepper
1 rack of lamb, about 250g (9oz), chined and French trimmed
4 tsp grain mustard
150g (5½oz) fresh breadcrumbs

1 Preheat the oven to 180°C fan (200°C/gas 6).

2 Put the new potatoes in a pan of cold water. Bring to the boil and blanch for 4–5 minutes. Drain in a colander, then spread out on a baking tray. Scatter the sprigs of thyme and seasoning over the top. Roast for 15–25 minutes until the potatoes are tender, depending on their size.

3 Meanwhile, brush the fat side of the lamb rack with some of the grain mustard, then dip into the breadcrumbs to coat. Place the rack fat side up in a small roasting tin and roast for 10–15 minutes, depending on how well cooked you like lamb. Leave to rest for a few minutes before cutting into cutlets.

4 When the potatoes are ready, mix in the remaining mustard together with a drizzle of olive oil. Serve with the lamb.

I think that award-winning butcher Colin Robinson of Grassington, Skipton, has some of the best lamb in the country. I serve it at royal dinners. I've devised this recipe for Colin's meat.

LAMB CHOPS WITH STEWED BEANS AND ROSEMARY

serves 4

6 double rib lamb chops, chined, fat trimmed, and bones French trimmed
salt and pepper
2 tbsp olive oil
knob of butter
½ onion, diced
2 garlic cloves, chopped
2 sprigs of fresh thyme
2 sprigs of fresh rosemary
1 carrot, peeled and cut into small dice
200ml (7fl oz) chicken stock
400ml (14fl oz) lamb stock
½ leek, diced
175g (6oz) cooked or canned haricot or cannellini beans
75g (2½oz) podded broad beans, blanched and skinned
200g (7oz) green beans, blanched and cut in half
1 tomato, deseeded and diced

1 Preheat the oven to 180°C fan (200°C/gas 6).

2 Season the lamb. Heat 1 tbsp of the oil in a heavy ovenproof pan and brown the chops on both sides. Add the butter and melt it, then baste the chops gently. Transfer the pan to the oven and cook the chops for 5–7 minutes for rare, 8–9 minutes for medium-rare, and 10–12 minutes for well done. Remove from the oven and allow to rest.

3 While the lamb is cooking, heat the remaining olive oil in a frying pan and sweat the onion and garlic with the thyme and rosemary for a few minutes to soften. Add the carrot and then the chicken stock. Boil to reduce by half.

4 Pour in the lamb stock and reduce by half again. Add the leek, then mix in the white beans, broad beans, green beans, and tomato. Bring to the boil and cook for a few minutes. Season to taste.

5 Spoon the stewed beans onto warmed serving plates. Place the lamb on top to serve.

Over the years in the UK, we've made many dishes from other countries our own, adopting them into our national cuisine. One of these is Greek or Turkish moussaka, which is the inspiration for the recipe here.

LAMB-STUFFED AUBERGINES

serves 4

4 aubergines
olive oil
2 onions, chopped
2 garlic cloves, crushed
450g (1lb) minced lamb
4 plum tomatoes, diced
good pinch of ground cumin
good pinch of ground cinnamon
1 glass red wine
2 tbsp chopped fresh mint
100ml (3½fl oz) chicken stock
salt and pepper
2 eggs, beaten
pinch of freshly grated nutmeg
75g (2½oz) mozzarella cheese, grated
75g (2½oz) Cheddar cheese, grated

white sauce
15g (½oz) unsalted butter
15g (½oz) plain flour
300ml (10fl oz) milk

1 Preheat the oven to 190°C fan (210°C/gas 6½).

2 Cut the aubergines lengthways in half and carefully scoop out the flesh, keeping the skins intact; reserve the skins. Dice the aubergine flesh.

3 Heat a little olive oil in a frying pan, add the diced aubergine, onions, and garlic, and fry for a few minutes. Turn the heat up, add the lamb, and fry until it is browned, stirring to break up any lumps. Stir in the tomatoes. Add the cumin and cinnamon with the wine and sauté to break up the tomatoes. Stir in the chopped mint and chicken stock. Bring to the boil, then simmer for 4–5 minutes to reduce excess liquid. Season with salt and pepper. Remove from the heat.

4 To make the white sauce, melt the butter in a small saucepan and stir in the flour. Cook for 1–2 minutes, then gradually whisk in the milk. Heat gently and cook for a further 3–4 minutes, stirring constantly until thickened.

5 Spoon the lamb mixture into the aubergine skins and place them on a baking tray. Mix together the white sauce, eggs, nutmeg, and seasoning, and spoon evenly over the filling. Scatter the mixed grated cheeses on top. Bake for 20–25 minutes until the filling is bubbling hot and the top is golden brown. Serve immediately.

Sherie Plumb won the runner bean and pickling shallot classes at Wimpole Hall. She says, "The night before a show is usually hectic, but the family still expect a good nutritious meal, so I often do lasagne. It can be prepared earlier in the day, ready to cook when required".

SHERIE PLUMB'S LASAGNE

serves 4

a little vegetable oil
1 medium onion or a few
   shallots, sliced
450g (1lb) minced beef
4 tomatoes, skinned
   and chopped
2 tbsp tomato ketchup or
   tomato purée
dash of Worcestershire sauce
1 tsp dried mixed herbs
salt and pepper
1 medium aubergine,
   sliced thinly
4 courgettes, sliced thinly
115g (4oz) lasagne sheets
   (no-need-to-cook type)

white sauce
30g (1oz) plain flour
30g (1oz) margarine
600ml (1 pint) milk
115g (4oz) Cheddar cheese,
   grated

topping
55g (2oz) Cheddar cheese,
   grated

1 Put a little oil into a saucepan, add the onion and minced beef, and put a lid on the pan. Leave to sweat over a low heat, stirring occasionally, for 5–10 minutes until the onion is translucent and the meat no longer red.

2 Add the tomatoes, tomato ketchup, Worcestershire sauce, mixed herbs, and a little water. Season to taste. Leave to simmer for 10–15 minutes.

3 Meanwhile, make the white sauce. Put the flour, fat, and milk into a saucepan and cook over a low heat until thickened; stir constantly, otherwise you will get lumps. Season. Away from the heat, add the cheese and stir well.

4 Preheat the oven to 160°C fan (180°C/gas 4).

5 Put all the aubergine slices on the bottom of a 25 x 30cm (10 x 12in) ovenproof dish. Cover with the courgettes and season, then add half the meat mixture. Lay half the lasagne sheets on top and pour over half of the sauce. Cover with the rest of the meat mixture, then the rest of lasagne sheets, and finish with the remaining sauce. Sprinkle with the cheese.

6 Bake in the middle of the oven until bubbling and golden brown. Serve hot.

tip   Although advice for modern varieties say it's not necessary, I still think it best to extract some of the bitterness from aubergines. After slicing, put them into a dish, sprinkle them with salt, and leave for 30 minutes, then rinse well before using them.

Sherie says, "After a long day at a show, everyone is starving and wants a meal ASAP. One thing we have here is plenty of vegetables — five a day is no problem in this house. This recipe is a favourite, one that children can help to prepare whatever their age".

S.A.S.S.F (SHERIE'S AFTER-SHOW STIR-FRY)

serves 4

a little vegetable oil
small knob of butter
    (optional – for better taste)
a few shallots, cut into quarters
2 carrots, peeled and cut into
    5cm (2in) lengths, then
    into matchsticks
4 boneless chicken breasts,
    skinned and cut into strips
salt and pepper
225g (8oz) runner beans, cut
    into 2.5cm (1in) chunks
1 small cauliflower, broken
    into florets
4 courgettes, sliced thinly
a little soy sauce

1 Heat the oil and butter in a large wok. Add the shallots and stir-fry for 2 minutes. Add the carrots and fry for 4 minutes, stirring occasionally.

2 Add the chicken and season, then stir-fry for 4–5 minutes until slightly browning on the edges. Add the runner beans and cook for a further 3 minutes.

3 Add the cauliflower florets, put a lid on wok, and cook for 5 minutes, stirring occasionally. Add the courgettes, put the lid on again, and sweat, stirring occasionally, for 4 minutes until all the vegetables are tender.

4 Adjust the seasoning, add a dash of soy sauce, and stir, then serve. Delicious.

tip   Don't forget that runner beans came from rainforests originally. They appreciate lots of water when they're growing, especially down their leaves in hot weather. That way they'll grow quickly and be very tender, with no strings.

Grapes are a classic garnish with chicken. Here I've used poussins, which are baby chickens. For this recipe they are "butterflied" – boned out and then opened flat like a book (ask your butcher to do this for you).

ROAST POUSSIN WITH RISOTTO AND GRAPES

serves 4

olive oil
4 small poussins, boned
  and butterflied
salt and pepper

risotto
2 tbsp olive oil
85g (3oz) unsalted butter
1 leek, white part only, diced
4 shallots, sliced
2 garlic cloves, sliced
300g (10½oz) risotto rice
250ml (8fl oz) white wine
1.5 litres (2¾ pints) chicken
  stock, heated to simmering
75g (2½oz) Parmesan cheese,
  freshly grated
juice of 1 lemon

grapes
140g (5oz) small seedless
  grapes
a handful of small fresh
  basil leaves
good splash of extra virgin
  olive oil
splash of apple juice
black pepper

1 Preheat the oven to 180°C fan (200°C/gas 6).

2 Drizzle some oil over the bottom of a large ovenproof pan (or two medium pans) and heat over a high heat until smoking. Season the poussins, then sear skin side down in the hot pan for 3–4 minutes. Turn them over and transfer the pan to the oven. Roast for 15 minutes until cooked through. When they are done, remove from the oven and set aside to rest.

3 While the poussins are cooking, make the risotto. Heat the olive oil and half the butter in a saucepan over a medium heat and gently sauté the leek, shallots, and garlic until tender, without colouring. Add the rice and stir until it is well coated with oil and butter. Reduce the heat to low and stir in the wine. Cook until the wine is almost completely absorbed by the rice, stirring frequently. Add 250ml (8fl oz) of the hot stock and cook until it is almost all absorbed, still stirring frequently. Continue adding stock and stirring in this way until it has all been absorbed. At the end of cooking, the rice should be al dente (tender, but a bit firm in the centre) and the risotto creamy.

4 When the risotto is nearly ready, combine the grapes with the basil, extra virgin olive oil, apple juice, and a good grind of black pepper. Add to the poussins and heat for 1–2 minutes.

5 Fold the Parmesan and remaining butter through the risotto. Season to taste with salt, pepper, and lemon juice.

6 To serve, divide the risotto among warmed serving bowls, place a poussin on top, and spoon over the grape mixture.

I have to confess that when my chef, Chris, and I were testing the recipes for this book, I ate the whole of this pie. It is brilliant. I loved it so much we made it again so I could share a slice with my dog, Fudge.

CHICKEN, LEEK, AND TARRAGON PIE

serves 8–10

filling
1 free-range chicken, about 1.5kg (3lb 3oz)
1 carrot, peeled and roughly chopped
2 celery sticks, roughly chopped
2 onions, finely chopped
6–8 sprigs of fresh tarragon
salt and pepper
1 tbsp olive oil
knob of butter
2 leeks, finely sliced
150ml (5fl oz) white wine
2 tbsp plain flour
150ml (5fl oz) single cream
grated zest of ½ lemon

pastry
600g (1¼lb) rich shortcrust pastry, home-made or bought
beaten egg to glaze

tip Leaving the chicken to cool in the stock helps to keep it moist. Reduce the remaining chicken stock further and freeze for another use.

1 Place the chicken in a large pan with the carrot, celery, half the onions, and 3–4 tarragon sprigs. Season and cover with water. Bring to the boil and simmer for 45 minutes until the chicken is cooked through. Remove from the heat and cool, then lift out the chicken and set aside. Return the stock to the hob and simmer for a further 30 minutes until reduced by half.

2 Heat the oil and butter in a large frying pan, add the leeks and remaining onion, and gently cook for 5 minutes until soft. Turn up the heat, add the wine, and cook for 3–4 minutes until reduced by half. Add the flour and stir well for 1 minute. Stir in the cream, 150ml (5fl oz) of the reduced chicken stock, the lemon zest, and seasoning. Remove from the heat.

3 Take the meat from the cooled chicken and chop or shred into small pieces, discarding all the skin and bones. Add the chicken meat and the remaining tarragon, chopped, to the leek and cream mixture and stir together. Set aside to cool.

4 Preheat the oven to 180°C fan (200°C/gas 6). Place a baking tray in the oven to heat.

5 Roll out two-thirds of the pastry on a floured surface and use to line a 23cm (9in) round pie tin. Fill with the chicken mixture. Brush the edges of the pastry case with beaten egg. Roll out the remaining pastry to make a lid, lay it over the filling, and crimp the edges to seal. Trim away excess pastry and brush the lid with beaten egg to glaze. Place on the hot baking tray. Bake for 40–45 minutes until the pastry is golden and crisp.

Always popular with the crowds, the enormous leeks dwarf their culinary counterparts on the showbench. Head Judge Medwyn Williams advises, "To grow large leeks, you need either unrooted 'pips' or 'grass' from a reputable pot leek grower or young seedlings that have been grown on from 'pips' or 'grass'".

THE HEAVIEST LEEK

Head Judge Medwyn Williams

"Have your soil analysed by a reputable soil analyst who will then recommend which nutrients and how much, if any, to add to your soil prior to soil preparation. Do not be tempted to overfeed your leeks with nitrogenous fertilizers; if they are growing away well with a lovely green colour, leave them well alone. Do not leave them to get stressed out by being too cold, too hot, having too much water or not enough."

Judge Gerald Treweek

"Leeks need starting off early. The top exhibitors only use 'grass' or 'bulbils', which appear on the leek seed head. These are set off in the greenhouse in early November, potted on until April and then set out in a plastic tunnel."

Judge John Trim

"For eating, I can honestly say I have never come across a bad variety of leek. Most of the older types are of the open pollinated varieties. When scanning the seed catalogue the only thing to consider is season of use, and choose accordingly. My own favourites are Prize taker, The Lyon and the F1 variety Snowdon." (See pages 216–217 for more information on varieties.)

Clive Bevan at The Great British
Village Show at Wimpole Hall

Butchers in the UK are now diversifying to satisfy our adventurous tastes. One I met in Wales had made some super stuff, like his own Parma ham and biltong. This recipe uses pancetta, which is of course Italian, but good-quality thin, streaky bacon rashers are good too.

BREAST OF CHICKEN WITH PANCETTA AND CREAMED LEEKS

serves 4

4 chicken breasts, French
   trimmed (ask your butcher
   to do this)
knob of butter
12 slices of pancetta

leeks
knob of butter
1 small white onion, diced
1 garlic clove, crushed
4 leeks, diced
2 sprigs of fresh thyme
4 tbsp white wine
150ml (5fl oz) double cream
salt and pepper
1 tbsp chopped fresh parsley

1 Preheat the oven to 200°C fan (220°C/gas 7).

2 First prepare the leeks. Heat a saucepan, add the butter, and sauté the onion and garlic for 2–3 minutes. Stir in the leeks and thyme, then add the white wine followed by the cream. Bring to the boil and simmer for 10 minutes.

3 Meanwhile, fry the chicken breasts in butter for 3–4 minutes on each side. Transfer them to a baking tray and top with slices of pancetta. Bake for 15–20 minutes, until cooked through.

4 Season the leeks and stir in the parsley. Spoon onto the warmed plates, top with the chicken breasts, and serve.

tip   A French-trimmed chicken breast is boned, but the cleaned wing bone is left attached. You can use boneless chicken breasts instead.

A butcher told me that Aylesbury ducks were becoming less popular than Gressingham. That's such a shame, especially considering he was from Oxford. Whichever duck you use, I recommend that you cook it pink as otherwise it will become tough.

SAVOY CABBAGE WITH ROAST DUCK BREAST

serves 4

4 duck breasts
salt and pepper
olive oil, for frying

cabbage
1 medium Savoy cabbage
2 star anise
3½ tbsp olive oil
1 glass white wine
2 sprigs of fresh thyme
3 garlic cloves, crushed
4 shallots, thinly sliced
150ml (5fl oz) beef stock

1 Preheat the oven to 200°C fan (220°C/gas 7).

2 Score the skin side of the duck breasts with a sharp knife, cutting through the fat but not into the meat, and season with salt and pepper. Heat a little olive oil in a non-stick ovenproof pan and put in the duck breasts skin side down. Fry for 6–7 minutes, then turn them over. Transfer the pan to the oven and cook for 5–6 minutes for pink, or 10–12 minutes for well done. When the duck is cooked, remove from the pan and allow to rest for about 4 minutes.

3 While the duck is cooking, prepare the cabbage. Remove the three large outer leaves from the cabbage and discard. Cut out the core, then thinly slice the cabbage.

4 Put the star anise and olive oil in a saucepan and warm through. Add the sliced cabbage and toss on a low heat for a few minutes to soften. Pour in the white wine and reduce by half, then add the thyme, garlic, and shallots, and mix well. Finally, add the beef stock and bring to the boil. Season, then remove from the heat.

5 Drain the cabbage in a sieve set over a bowl. Spoon the cabbage onto warmed plates. Slice the duck breasts and arrange on top, then pour over the cabbage cooking liquid.

True chicory is a flowering plant — endive (confusingly called chicory in the UK) is the stuff you need for this dish. It has a slightly bitter aftertaste and is mainly used in salads. But braising and chargrilling it to serve with meats and fish works really well.

HONEYED DUCK BREAST WITH CHICORY

serves 4

chicory
4 heads of chicory
1 head of radicchio
100ml (3½fl oz) white wine
250ml (8fl oz) orange juice
50g (1¾oz) caster sugar
1 tbsp chopped fresh coriander
salt and pepper
butter

duck
4 tbsp clear honey
4 large duck breasts, preferably Gressingham
3 sprigs of fresh thyme
red wine sauce (see page 117) heated to serve

1 Preheat the oven to 200°C fan (220°C/gas 7).

2 Cut the chicory and radicchio heads lengthways in half and place in a shallow roasting tin. Drizzle over the white wine and orange juice, and sprinkle with the sugar, coriander, and seasoning. Cover with foil and bake for 20 minutes until tender.

3 Meanwhile, cook the duck breasts. Heat a heavy ovenproof frying pan on the stovetop with the honey. Season the breasts, then place fat side down in the pan. Fry for 6–7 minutes to brown them well, then turn over. Add the thyme sprigs and transfer to the oven. Roast for 8 minutes for rare; 10 minutes for medium; 12 minutes for well done. When the duck is cooked to your taste, remove it from the oven and allow to rest for a few minutes.

4 Drain the chicory and, if you like, chargrill it. Heat a griddle or ridged grill pan and colour the chicory nicely.

5 To serve, place the chicory and radicchio in the centre of the warmed plates. Slice the duck breasts and arrange on top, then spoon the red wine sauce around the edge.

The Great British Village Show
Calke Abbey, Derbyshire

If you're looking for the sort of countryside the Englishman dreams of when he's far from home, you couldn't do much better than this part of the country around Calke Abbey. The results of months of toil on the vegetable patch and hours of slaving over a hot stove were placed on the showbenches in an attempt to wow the judges and win a place in the final. Two neighbours and long-standing rivals fought it out in the giant leek class, and children from Eureka Primary School in Swadlincote brought along produce they had grown themselves on their new allotment.

Now, I'm no Alan Titchmarsh, but courgettes have got to be the easiest thing to grow in the garden. It gives you the chance to have the flowers too. If you go to any market in Italy, you will always see courgettes and their flowers, which are great deep-fried in tempura batter.

SAUTÉED COURGETTES WITH SESAME AND SOY SAUCE, AND DUCK CONFIT

serves 4

4 duck legs confit (see Potted Duck and Pork, page 46)
fresh chervil to garnish

haricot dressing
6 tbsp extra virgin olive oil
1–2 tbsp white wine vinegar
salt and pepper
1 can (about 400g) haricot or cannellini beans, packed in water, drained

courgettes
4 tsp olive oil
4 tsp toasted sesame oil
2 shallots, thinly sliced
400g (14oz) courgettes, sliced thinly lengthways, then cut into matchsticks
4 tsp soy sauce
2 tsp toasted sesame seeds

1 Preheat the oven to 180°C fan (200°C/gas 6).

2 Place the duck legs with their fat in a small roasting dish and heat in the oven for about 20 minutes, basting regularly with the melted fat.

3 Meanwhile, make the haricot dressing. Whisk together the oil, vinegar, and seasoning in a bowl to combine. Put the haricot beans in a saucepan and gently warm through. Add the vinaigrette and warm for a further 1–2 minutes. Remove from the heat and set aside.

4 To prepare the courgettes, heat the olive and sesame oils in a non-stick pan over a medium heat. Add the shallots and cook for 1–2 minutes, then add the matchstick courgettes and fry quite quickly for a further 2 minutes, stirring well. When the courgettes start to soften, add the soy sauce and stir to mix, then stir in the toasted sesame seeds. Season with pepper and remove from the heat.

5 To serve, place the duck legs confit skin side up in four large, shallow bowls. Put the warm courgettes on top, spoon over the dressing, and garnish with chervil.

Sorrel is an easy herb to grow. It is great in salads, although as it has a slightly bitter taste it is best used with other leaves. If you are cooking it, as in the sauce here, add it at the last minute because the leaves will go brown very quickly.

ESCALOPES OF SALMON WITH SORREL SAUCE

serves 4

salmon
750g (1lb 10oz) salmon fillet, taken from a good-sized salmon
2 tbsp sunflower oil
salt and pepper

sauce
600ml (1 pint) fish stock
175ml (6fl oz) double cream
4 tbsp dry vermouth, such as Noilly Prat
75g (2½oz) unsalted butter
2 tsp lemon juice
200g (7oz) frozen peas
25g (scant 1oz) sorrel leaves, thinly sliced

1 Preheat the grill to high.

2 Cut the salmon fillet into 12 slices or escalopes. Brush each one with oil and season with salt, then lay them side by side on a lightly oiled baking tray. Set aside.

3 For the sauce, put the fish stock, half of the cream, and the vermouth in a large saucepan and boil vigorously until reduced to about 175ml (6fl oz). Add the remaining cream, the butter, and lemon juice, and simmer until slightly thickened to a good sauce consistency. Stir in the peas and season to taste. When hot, remove from the heat and keep warm.

4 Grill the salmon escalopes for about 30 seconds to 1 minute until only just firm.

5 Stir most of the sorrel into the sauce. Spoon the sauce into the centre of the warmed plates. Arrange three escalopes, slightly overlapping, on top of the sauce on each plate and sprinkle with the remaining sorrel. Serve immediately.

Farmed sea bass normally weighs less than line-caught fish. Try to use line-caught fish for this if you can. Get the fishmonger to scale the fish for you when he guts it, as it's a bit of a pain to do this yourself.

STUFFED SEA BASS WITH ONIONS, HERBS, AND HONEY

serves 2–4

olive oil
2 large white onions, sliced
2 garlic cloves, sliced
2 tbsp runny honey
dash of white wine vinegar
salt and pepper
1 whole sea bass, about
   450g (1lb), scaled and gutted
1 bay leaf
1 sprig of fresh rosemary
1 sprig of fresh thyme

1 Preheat the oven to 190°C fan (210°C/gas 6½).

2 Heat a little oil in a pan and fry the onions and garlic until soft. Add the honey and white wine vinegar and cook until the onions are golden brown. Season and allow to cool.

3 Score the skin on the fish on both sides with a sharp knife and season generously with salt and pepper. Drizzle over some olive oil and rub into the skin. Stuff the fish with the onions and herbs and place on a greased baking tray.

4 Bake for about 20 minutes or until cooked. Serve the sea bass hot, with a leafy green salad.

This dish is so simple, yet for me it is one of the best in the whole book. The secret is to cook the carrots quickly at the end, so that the water evaporates and leaves a great glaze coating them.

PAN-FRIED HALIBUT WITH GLAZED CARROTS

serves 4

500g (1lb 2oz) skinless
   halibut fillet
salt and pepper
500ml (17fl oz) water or
   vegetable stock
25g (scant 1oz) sugar
50g (1¾oz) butter
500g (1lb 2oz) baby carrots
3½ tbsp olive oil
25g (scant 1oz) fresh flat-leaf
   parsley, chopped
25g (scant 1oz) fresh chervil,
   chopped

1 Divide the halibut fillet into four even pieces and season them. Set aside.

2 Put the water or stock, sugar, 1 tsp salt, and the butter in a saucepan. Add the carrots. Bring to the boil, then cover with a lid and turn down the heat. Leave to simmer.

3 Heat a non-stick frying pan, add the olive oil, and place the halibut in the pan. When the underside of the fish starts to brown (after 2–4 minutes), turn the pieces over and cook for another 2–4 minutes. Remove from the heat.

4 The pan of carrots should have only a small amount of liquid left. Remove the lid and boil on a high heat to reduce the liquid to a syrupy glaze, then add the chopped herbs and stir gently. Serve the carrots with the halibut.

Clams are a bit like Marmite — you either love them or hate them. I think if you get them fresh they have the most amazing flavour. Treat them like mussels, cleaning well and throwing out any that don't open after cooking.

JERUSALEM ARTICHOKE AND CLAM RISOTTO

serves 4

50g (1¾oz) butter, diced
olive oil, for frying
400g (14oz) Jerusalem
   artichokes, peeled and cut
   into 2cm (¾in) dice
salt and pepper
2 shallots, chopped
2 garlic cloves, chopped
225g (8oz) risotto rice
17fl oz (500ml) simmering
   chicken stock, or more
   if needed
100ml (3½fl oz) white wine
12 large, fresh clams
1–2 tbsp chopped fresh
   flat-leaf parsley
2 tbsp mascarpone
75g (2½oz) Parmesan cheese,
   freshly grated

1 Heat half the butter with a little olive oil in a frying pan and sauté the artichokes with a little salt and pepper for about 20 minutes until tender.

2 Meanwhile, sweat the shallots and garlic in the rest of the butter in a saucepan until soft, without colouring. Stir in the rice, then add a ladleful of stock. Gently simmer, stirring frequently, until the stock is almost all absorbed, then add another ladleful. Continue cooking, adding the stock gradually and stirring frequently, until all the stock has been absorbed.

3 While the risotto is cooking, heat a large pan and add the white wine and clams. Cover tightly with a lid and cook briskly for 1–2 minutes until the clams are open. Drain off the liquid and add it to the rice. Reserve the clams for garnish.

4 At the end of cooking the rice should be al dente (tender but still a bit firm in the centre) and the risotto creamy. Add extra stock if necessary. Add half the parsley to the risotto, together with the mascarpone and half the grated Parmesan. Season well and stir in the artichokes. Spoon the risotto onto warmed plates and garnish with the clams and remaining chopped parsley and Parmesan. Drizzle over some olive oil and serve.

My chef, Chris, and I came up with the idea for this bitter-sweet salad. It works fab with tuna steaks and also with grilled chicken breast.

SEARED TUNA STEAKS WITH GRAPE AND DANDELION SALAD

serves 4

salad
100g (3½oz) red grapes, cut in half
100g (3½oz) white grapes, cut in half
handful of dandelion leaves
handful of frisée leaves

dressing
3 tbsp extra virgin olive oil
3 tbsp vegetable or sunflower oil
1 tsp Chardonnay or other white wine vinegar
1 tsp grain mustard
squeeze of lime juice
squeeze of lemon juice
salt and pepper

fish
olive oil
4 tuna steaks
4 lemon wedges

1 To make the salad, toss the red and white grapes in a bowl with the dandelion and frisée leaves. Set aside until required.

2 For the dressing, whisk all the ingredients and seasoning together in a small bowl. Just before serving, drizzle over the salad and toss together.

3 Drizzle oil over the bottom of a griddle pan or ridged grill pan and heat until hot. Season the tuna steaks with salt and pepper, then chargrill to taste: 2 minutes on each side for pink, or 3–4 minutes on each side for well done. While the fish is cooking, add the lemon wedges to the pan and allow them to heat through and caramelize.

4 Divide the grape and dandelion salad among the serving plates and place the tuna alongside. Serve with the caramelized lemon wedges.

This year, my runner beans didn't grow as well in the garden as the French ones. I think runners should be served just with butter and black pepper, but French beans are good in other dishes, like this one. I did have a glut of French beans, though, which I like to pickle.

PICKLED FRENCH BEANS WITH PAN-FRIED RED MULLET FILLETS

serves 4

8 red mullet fillets, scaled and pin boned

pickled beans
olive oil
5 shallots, finely sliced
2 sprigs of fresh thyme, chopped
1 bay leaf
2 garlic cloves, crushed
1 small knob of fresh ginger, peeled and finely chopped
2 tsp pink peppercorns, crushed
450ml (15fl oz) white wine vinegar
500g (1lb 2oz) French beans, topped
75g (2½oz) caster sugar

1 To prepare the beans, heat a splash of oil in a heavy saucepan and sweat the shallots with the thyme, bay leaf, garlic, ginger, and peppercorns until soft, without colouring. Pour in the vinegar and stir well, then remove from the heat. Set aside to cool.

2 Bring a pan of lightly salted water to the boil and blanch the beans for 2 minutes. Drain and refresh in iced water.

3 Toss the beans with the sugar in a bowl, then pour over the cooled vinegar solution. Transfer to a sterilized preserving jar and seal. (The beans can be kept for 2–3 weeks in the fridge.)

4 Heat a non-stick frying pan. When hot, place the fish fillets skin side down in the pan and cook for 2–3 minutes until golden brown. Turn over and cook for a further 3 minutes.

5 Arrange a pile of drained beans on each plate and place the mullet fillets on top. Drizzle with olive oil and serve with new potatoes or salad leaves.

tip When you place the mullet fillets in the pan, gently press down using a fish slice, to prevent them from curling up too much.

Mackerel is one of those fish that's so cheap to buy, but must be as fresh as possible and simply cooked. Celery goes really well with mackerel.

MACKEREL PARCELS WITH CELERY AND PANCETTA

serves 4

1 tbsp olive oil
1 medium onion, diced
2 garlic cloves, crushed
100g (3½oz) pancetta cubes
  or smoked bacon lardons
4 celery sticks, each cut
  into thirds
4 whole mackerel, heads
  removed, scaled, and gutted
salt and pepper
few sprigs of fresh thyme
few sprigs of fresh flat-leaf
  parsley
2 lemons, cut into quarters
white wine

1 Preheat the oven to 180°C fan (200°C/gas 6).

2 Heat the oil in a non-stick frying pan and sauté the onion and garlic for 2–3 minutes to soften. Add the pancetta to the pan and fry until browned. Remove from the heat.

3 Cut out four large sheets of foil and greaseproof paper. Lay them on a flat surface, the paper on top of the foil. Divide the onion mixture into four portions and spread onto the centre of each sheet of greaseproof. Arrange the celery pieces on top. Season the mackerel and place on the celery. Scatter the thyme and parsley sprigs over the fish and add 2 lemon quarters to each one. Fold up the sides of the foil and greaseproof, then add a generous glug of wine to each parcel. Finally, fold over the top to close the parcel securely.

4 Place the parcels on a baking tray. Bake for 15–20 minutes until the fish is cooked through. Serve hot, in the parcels.

You can't beat fresh fish cakes for satisfaction. The cloves here add an extra dimension and these are fantastic with the pickled cucumber on the next page.

FISH CAKES

serves 6

fish
350g (12oz) undyed smoked
  haddock fillets
225g (8oz) salmon fillet
about 500ml (17fl oz) milk
1 onion, quartered
1 carrot, peeled and chopped
1 bay leaf
few black peppercorns
2 cloves

cakes
2 small onions, finely diced
200g (7oz) butter
350g (12oz) mashed potatoes
  without milk and butter
1 tbsp anchovy essence
4 hard-boiled eggs, chopped
  or grated (optional)
3 tbsp chopped fresh parsley
2 tbsp chopped fresh dill
salt and pepper
75g (2½oz) plain flour
2 eggs, beaten
150g (5½oz) natural
  breadcrumbs
olive oil, for frying

1 Put the haddock and salmon in a pan with enough milk to cover, the onion, carrot, bay leaf, peppercorns, and cloves. Bring to a simmer and poach for 5–6 minutes until cooked. Remove from the milk (reserve this). When cool enough to handle, flake the fish, discarding any skin or bone, and keeping the haddock separate from the salmon.

2 Soften the diced onions in 15g (½oz) of the butter, then cool. Melt 85g (3oz) of the remaining butter. Combine the haddock with the potato, onions, melted butter, and anchovy essence, either in an electric mixer fitted with a dough hook or using a spoon. Fold in the salmon, hard-boiled eggs, if using, parsley, and dill until well combined; do not overmix. Season to taste. If the mixture seems too dry, add some of the haddock poaching milk. Divide the mixture into six equal portions, then shape into patties. Refrigerate to set.

3 Dust the fish cakes with the flour, dip in the egg, and finally coat with breadcrumbs. Refrigerate to firm up, then fry in the remaining butter and a little olive oil for 5 minutes on each side until piping hot and golden brown. Serve the fish cakes hot, with the pickled cucumber.

The one big success I had in my greenhouse was the cucumbers. Don't get me wrong though. There were no champion whoppers, just juicy ripe cucs full of flavour.

PICKLED CUCUMBER

serves 6

pickled cucumber
1 cucumber
25g (scant 1oz) sea salt
4 tbsp groundnut oil
2 small dried red chillies
2.5cm (1in) piece fresh ginger, peeled and cut into fine shreds
1 fresh red chilli, deseeded and cut into fine shreds
5 tbsp rice wine vinegar
15g (½oz) caster sugar
1½ tsp pink peppercorns, crushed

1 Peel the cucumber, cut it in half lengthways, and scoop out the seeds, then cut into matchsticks. Sprinkle the cucumber with the salt and allow to stand for 1 hour. Rinse the cucumber and squeeze out any excess moisture.

2 Heat the oil in a wok or frying pan and add the dried chillies. Stir until they are blackened, then remove from the heat. Add the ginger, fresh chilli, vinegar, sugar, and peppercorns. Stir in the cucumber, then leave to cool. This pickle can be used straightaway, but if possible, pack into sterilized jars, seal, and leave to marinate for 3 days. Serve with the fish cakes opposite.

tip Any leftover pickled cucumber can be stored in an airtight container in the fridge for up to 5 days.

Here is a real blast of summer. The fresh herb sauce is based on a French classic, and is perfect with salmon. Served outdoors when the sun is shining, you could be anywhere in the world.

PAN-FRIED SALMON WITH TOMATO AND HERB SAUCE

serves 2

25g (scant 1oz) butter
olive oil
2 tail portions of salmon fillet,
   skin on, about 200g
   (7oz) each

sauce
2 plum tomatoes, deseeded
   and diced
¼ red onion, finely chopped
½ garlic clove, finely chopped
100ml (3½fl oz) olive oil
grated zest and juice of
   1 lemon
20g (¾oz) mixed fresh herbs
   (dill, tarragon, basil, chives,
   and flat-leaf parsley)
sea salt and pepper

1 To make the sauce, combine the tomatoes, onion, garlic, olive oil, lemon zest and juice, and chopped herbs in a saucepan. Set aside.

2 Heat up a non-stick frying pan and add the butter and a little olive oil. Pan-fry the salmon, skin side down, for 2 minutes to give a nice colour. Turn the fish over to cook the other side for 1–2 minutes. Remove from the heat and leave the fish in the pan for another 1–2 minutes to finish cooking. Meanwhile, warm the sauce and season it.

3 To serve, spoon the sauce onto warmed plates and set the pan-fried salmon on top.

Jan Kisiel won both the tomato class and the longest carrot class at the Petworth show. This is his courgette bake recipe, which you can make to please yourself, with varying amounts and optional extra ingredients.

JAN KISIEL'S COURGETTE BAKE

main ingredients
olive oil
onion, chopped
garlic cloves, crushed
courgettes/marrows/squash
  – any mixture, chopped
  or sliced
tomatoes, chopped
  (canned tomatoes can be
  used if you do not have fresh)
salt and pepper
Cheddar cheese, grated

extra ingredients (optional)
bacon, chopped
carrots, peeled and chopped
pasta, cooked

1 Heat some olive oil in pan and add the onion and garlic. If using bacon and carrots, add them now also. Cook, stirring occasionally, for about 10 minutes.

2 Add courgettes/marrows/squash and cook until soft, adding tomatoes and seasoning as you go. Stir in pasta, if using.

3 Layer up the courgette mix and cheese in an ovenproof dish until all is used, ending with a cheese layer. Bake or grill until golden brown on top.

Clive Bevan won the heaviest leek class at The Great British Village Show at Wimpole Hall. Here is his leek pie recipe, which will taste second to none.

CLIVE BEVAN'S LEEK PIE

4 bacon rashers
675g (1½lb) leeks, cut into small pieces
150ml (5fl oz) milk
150ml (5fl oz) single cream
2 large eggs
salt and pepper
280g (10oz) readymade shortcrust pastry
grated or finely crumbled blue cheese for the topping

1 Preheat the oven to 200°C fan (220°C/gas 7).

2 Grill the bacon rashers, then chop into small pieces.

3 Cook the leeks in simmering salted water for 10 minutes until soft. Drain well and place in a shallow ovenproof dish with the bacon.

4 Beat the milk, cream, and eggs together. Season and pour over the leeks.

5 Roll out the pastry and cover the dish. Make a slit in the top to allow the steam to escape during cooking. Put the grated or crumbled cheese on top.

6 Bake for 20 minutes. Reduce the temperature to 150°C fan (170°C/gas 3) and bake for a further 20 minutes. The reduction of the heat ensures that the filling does not become too hot, which could make it curdle. Serve hot.

The cauliflower is part of the cabbage family, believe it or not. I like the plain white cauli, although there is also an amazing-looking variety called romanesco, which is lime-green and spiky – a bit like a chameleon's eye.

CAULIFLOWER RISOTTO

serves 4

30g (1oz) butter
1 shallot, chopped
1 garlic clove, crushed
2 sprigs of fresh thyme
250g (9oz) risotto rice
4 tbsp white wine
1 litre (1¾ pints) simmering
  vegetable stock
250g (9oz) diced cauliflower
100g (3½oz) mascarpone
100 g (3½oz) Parmesan
  cheese, freshly grated
1–2 tbsp chopped fresh chives
salt and pepper
olive oil for drizzling

1 Melt the butter in a saucepan and sweat the shallot and garlic with the thyme until soft, without colouring. Add the rice and stir for about 30 seconds over a low heat. Add the white wine and bubble for a further few seconds, then add a ladleful of stock. Gently simmer, stirring frequently, until the stock is almost all absorbed, then add another ladleful. Continue cooking, adding the stock gradually and stirring frequently, for about 16 minutes.

2 Add the diced cauliflower and cook for a further 6 minutes, gradually adding the remaining stock. At the end of cooking, the rice should be al dente (tender but still a bit firm in the centre) and the risotto creamy.

3 Mix the mascarpone, most of the Parmesan, and the chives into the risotto and season well. To serve, put the risotto onto the centre of warm plates and top with the rest of the grated Parmesan and a drizzle of olive oil.

tip If you're feeling extravagant, drizzle a little truffle oil over the risotto just before serving.

This is kind of like an upmarket mash. It's great for a dinner party although it's also fab with sausages. Don't worry about truffle oil being expensive – a little bit goes an awfully long way as it's really strong.

POTATO AND HARICOT MASH WITH TRUFFLE OIL

serves 4–6

900g (2lb) large floury potatoes,
   preferably Maris Piper,
   peeled and quartered
420g (15oz) cooked or canned
   haricot or cannellini beans
100ml (3½fl oz) single cream
   or milk
75g (2½oz) unsalted butter
salt and pepper
freshly grated nutmeg
3 tbsp white truffle oil

1 Cook the potatoes in boiling salted water for 20–25 minutes until tender. Drain off all the water from the pan and replace the lid. Shake the pan vigorously, which will start to break up the boiled potatoes.

2 Add the beans and mash together well, then mash in the cream and butter. Season with salt, pepper, and nutmeg. Finally, beat in the truffle oil and serve.

tip For a smoother finish, pass the mashed potato and beans through a potato ricer or sieve, to remove the bean skins.

Gnocchi is an Italian dish, so you may be wondering what it's doing in a British cookery book. Well, the answer is that it's bloody good, especially when made with British spuds, which are the best of course. Sauté the gnocchi, then combine with some roast pumpkin and crumbled Stilton, and you'll have an amazing dish.

POTATO GNOCCHI

serves 4

900g (2lb) potatoes, preferably Maris Piper, scrubbed and pricked
175–200g (6–7oz) plain flour
3 egg yolks
1 tsp salt, or to taste
olive oil

tip You can keep the gnocchi, on a lightly floured tray in the fridge, for a few hours, or freeze them for several weeks and then cook from frozen.

1 Preheat the oven to 180°C fan (200°C/gas 6). Bake the potatoes for about 1 hour until completely cooked.

2 Split open the potatoes, scoop out the flesh, and press it through a potato ricer or sieve onto a board or work surface. Make a well in the centre. In it layer two-thirds of the flour with the egg yolks. Add the salt. Use a dough scraper to mix the potatoes quickly into the flour and eggs. Add more flour as needed to make a smooth dough. Shape into a ball.

3 Pull off a small piece of dough and roll into a ball about 1cm (½in) thick. Flatten slightly. Test for seasoning and texture by dropping it into a small pan of boiling salted water. It is cooked as soon as it floats to the surface. Add more salt to the dough if necessary, or a bit more flour if the test gnocchi seems mushy.

4 Pull off a portion of the remaining dough and roll it by hand on a lightly floured surface into a snake about 1cm (½in) thick. Cut into 1cm (½in) pieces, form balls, and roll the balls over the back of a fork to create oval gnocchi shapes. Continue forming gnocchi with the rest of the dough.

5 To cook, bring a large pan of salted water to the boil. Add the gnocchi. As they rise to the surface, use a slotted spoon to remove them to a bowl of iced water. Once they have cooled (about 2 minutes), drain briefly on kitchen paper or a tea towel.

6 To sauté the gnocchi, heat a film of olive oil in a frying pan over a medium to high heat. Toss in the gnocchi and cook for 1–2 minutes until golden brown on the underside. Serve hot.

Béarnaise is the classic sauce for steak. The secret to making the sauce thicken is to be sure the butter is bubbling when it is added to the egg yolks. Take care not to add the butter too quickly.

BÉARNAISE SAUCE

serves 4

3 tbsp tarragon vinegar
3½ tbsp white wine or water
1 tsp crushed white
   peppercorns
175g (6oz) unsalted butter
4 egg yolks
pinch of caster sugar
1–2 tbsp chopped fresh
   tarragon
½ lemon
salt and pepper

1 Heat the vinegar and wine or water with the peppercorns in a pan and bring to the boil. Simmer rapidly until the liquid has reduced by half. Strain out the peppercorns, then return the liquid to the pan and bring back to the boil.

2 In another pan, gently melt the butter. Add the reduced liquid and bring to a rolling boil.

3 Place the egg yolks in a blender and blitz, then with the motor running, slowly pour in the hot vinegar and butter mixture in a thin stream through the hole in the lid.

4 Pour the sauce into a bowl and leave for 3 minutes, stirring occasionally. If the sauce has not thickened enough, pour it back into the pan and stir constantly over the lowest possible heat until it thickens.

5 Add the sugar, chopped tarragon, and a squeeze of lemon juice. Season to taste. Serve warm.

A simple red wine sauce is great with all kinds of savoury dishes, including sausages with white bean mash (see page 68) and roast belly of pork with root vegetables (see page 64).

RED WINE SAUCE

serves 4

375ml (13fl oz) red wine
1 litre (1¾ pints) brown
    chicken stock

1 Place the wine in a pan and bring to the boil. Allow it to reduce by half.

2 Add the chicken stock and continue to reduce on a rapid boil until only about one-third of the original quantity is left. Serve the sauce hot.

tip   To make a brown chicken stock, you need to roast the chicken pieces and bones first until well coloured, before adding the remaining ingredients, such as vegetables, herbs, and other flavourings.

3

puddings and pastries

Highgrove Black Butter Ice Cream   **Eton Mess with Orange Cordial**
Lemon Verbena Meringue with Mango and Passion Fruit   **Vanilla Castle
Pudding with Raspberry Jam**   Jam Roly-Poly   **Raspberry Cranachan**
Lemon and Treacle Tart   **Pear and Rosemary Crumble with Cinnamon
Sauce**   Upside-Down Pear and Mulberry Tart   **Almond Tart**   Apricot,
Ginger, and Custard Danish   **Jean Gallimore's Redcurrant Frangipan**
Hampshire Roll   **Yorkshire Curd Tart**   Eccles Cakes   **Sultana and
Treacle Toffee**

When you brown butter, it takes on a whole different flavour. It is often used to sauce fish. Here I've put it into a rich ice cream. The bitter hint stops the ice cream from being too sweet.

HIGHGROVE BLACK BUTTER ICE CREAM

serves 4

40g (1½oz) unsalted butter,
  preferably Highgrove
  butter, diced
300ml (10fl oz) milk
300ml (10fl oz) double cream
  (Jersey dairy)
120g (4oz) caster sugar
6 egg yolks

1 To make the black butter, heat a pan and, when hot, add the diced butter and stir until melted. Once the butter turns a nutty brown colour, strain through a sieve lined with muslin into a bowl and allow to cool.

2 Place the milk and cream in a pan and heat to a simmer. Add the black butter. Remove from the heat.

3 Beat the sugar with the egg yolks until pale and fluffy. Add the milk mixture to the egg yolks and sugar, whisking constantly. Pour into a clean pan and gently heat to 80°C, stirring all the time with a wooden spoon. The custard should be thick enough to coat the back of the spoon. Pour into a bowl and leave to cool.

4 When cold, place in ice-cream maker and churn until frozen.

5 Transfer to a suitable container, cover with cling film, and place in the freezer. Leave to set for 1–2 hours. Serve on its own or with some fresh fruit.

tip   If the ice cream comes straight from the freezer, leave it to stand at room temperature for 5–10 minutes before serving.

The 4th of June is the day that Eton Mess is traditionally served at Eton College. I put in some orange cordial, as orange brings out the flavour of strawberries.

ETON MESS WITH ORANGE CORDIAL

serves 4–6

500g (1lb 2oz) strawberries
400ml (14fl oz) double cream
3 meringue nests, about 7.5cm
  (3in) diameter, crushed
3½tbsp orange cordial

to garnish
strawberries
sprigs of fresh mint

1 Hull the strawberries, then purée half of them in a blender. Chop the remaining strawberries into small dice.

2 Whip the double cream until stiff. Fold in the strawberry purée and crushed meringue. Add the chopped strawberries and fold them in together with the orange cordial.

3 Divide among wine glasses. Garnish with strawberries and mint, then serve, or keep in the fridge for up to 2 hours.

In the past, verbena was used for perfumes, and if you rub a leaf and smell it you can see why. The flavour has a hint of citrus, which goes so well in desserts like this as well as creamy puds like crème caramel and brûlée.

LEMON VERBENA MERINGUE WITH MANGO AND PASSION FRUIT

serves 6

meringue
3 large egg whites
125g (4½oz) caster sugar
12 leaves of lemon verbena, chopped

filling
115g (4oz) fresh mango, diced
6 passion fruits
grated zest and juice of ½ orange
25g (scant 1oz) caster sugar

to finish
300ml (10fl oz) double cream
150g (5½oz) mascarpone or good cream cheese
1 vanilla pod, split open
25g (scant 1oz) pistachio nuts, toasted and lightly crushed
sifted icing sugar, to dust

1 Preheat the oven to 180°C fan (200°C/gas 6). Lay non-stick silicone liners on two baking sheets.

2 Whisk the egg whites in a large, clean bowl until they form stiff peaks, then whisk in the caster sugar, a little at a time. Fold in the lemon verbena. Divide the meringue mixture equally between the baking sheets and gently spread each portion into a 17.5cm (7in) round.

3 Bake the meringue rounds on the centre shelf of the oven for 5 minutes. Turn the oven off and leave the meringues inside to dry out for at least 4 hours.

4 For the filling, put the mango dice in a mixing bowl. Cut the passion fruits in half and scrape out the pulp and seeds into the bowl. Add the orange zest and juice and sugar. Mix together and set aside.

5 Whip the cream to soft peaks, then fold in the mascarpone and sticky seeds scraped from the vanilla pod. Carefully spread half the mixture over one of meringue rounds, then spoon the mango and passion fruit mixture over the cream. Place the other meringue on top. Spread the remaining cream mixture over it and decorate with the toasted pistachios. Dust with icing sugar to serve.

illustrated on pages 124–125

My gran used to make castle puddings when I was a kid. So when I bought a jar of jam from a WI stall, I couldn't resist making these when I got home.

VANILLA CASTLE PUDDING WITH RASPBERRY JAM

serves 6

175g (6oz) butter
150g (5oz) caster sugar
1 vanilla pod, split open
3 eggs
175g (6oz) plain flour
1 rounded tsp baking powder
a jar of the best raspberry jam
   you can find
1 normal size punnet of
   fresh raspberries

1 Preheat the oven to 180°C fan (200°C/gas 6). Grease six dariole moulds with a little butter.

2 Put the butter and caster sugar in a bowl. Scrape the sticky seeds from the vanilla pod into the bowl. Cream until soft and pale. Beat in the eggs one by one. Stir in the flour and baking powder until amalgamated.

3 Fill the moulds three-quarters full – any more and you will witness an eruption. Place the moulds on a baking tray and bake for 20–25 minutes until golden and risen. Loosen the puddings with a palette knife, then turn out onto plates.

4 Heat up the raspberry jam, then add the fresh raspberries. Pour copious quantities of the hot raspberries and jam over the puddings and serve.

tip Before turning out the puddings, cut off any uneven tops, so they will have flat bases to sit on.

I've heard this called dead man's arm pudding and shirtsleeve pudding, as it was often steamed in an old shirtsleeve — or so they say. Traditional desserts like this should be on more restaurant menus, but squeezy bottles of coulis have taken over. It's sad really because everyone loves British puds.

JAM ROLY-POLY

serves 4

230g (8oz) self-raising flour
1 tsp baking powder
pinch of salt
finely grated zest of 1 lemon
150g (5½oz) shredded suet
100–150ml (3½–5fl oz) milk
150–175g (5–6oz) raspberry
  jam

1 Mix together the self-raising flour, baking powder, and salt. Add the lemon zest and shredded suet, and rub together to make a breadcrumb consistency. Add the milk a little at a time to combine into a soft dough. Wrap in cling film and allow to rest in the fridge for 20–30 minutes.

2 Roll out the suet dough into a rectangle about 35 x 25cm (14 x 10in). Spread the jam evenly over the dough, leaving a clear 1cm (½in) border. Brush the border with extra milk or water, then roll up the dough from a wider edge, pinching at both ends to seal in all the jam. Wrap the roly-poly loosely in greaseproof paper, then loosely in foil, and tie securely with string at each end.

3 Steam the pudding in a steamer for 1½ hours, topping up with hot water during the cooking time as needed.

4 Unwrap, slice, and serve with ice cream or pouring cream.

The raspberry entries had a maximum points value of 12, which was broken down into four categories:
Condition 4 points
Size 3 points
Colour 3 points
Uniformity 2 points

In the raspberry class, plates of 12 fruits were presented by eager hopefuls for inspection by the judges. The raspberries were judged to rules laid down in The Royal Horticultural Society Show Handbook.

THE RASPBERRY CLASS

Head Judge Medwyn Williams
"The requirements of the schedule were for a dish of 12 large raspberries. They should be uniform in size, ripe, of good colour, with stalks attached and in good condition with no blemishes. Fruits that are 'hard-nosed' through imperfect fertilization or lacking stalks are defective for competition."

Judge Gerald Treweek
"Competition raspberries must have no insect damage or imperfect fertilization. They must have been grown by the competitor for at least 3 months and the number of fruit on the schedule must be adhered to."

Judge John Trim
"An outstanding variety of raspberry is Autumn Bliss. A sunny position is best to get the most luscious raspberries, and keep them well-watered once berries start to form."

This is such a simple Scottish dessert. The traditional way to serve it is to take all the ingredients separately to the table and let the guests help themselves and make their own pud. If you put it together, it can be eaten immediately or refrigerated for up to 2 hours.

RASPBERRY CRANACHAN

serves 4

75g (2½oz) medium oatmeal
4 tbsp raspberry jam (optional)
300ml (10fl oz) double cream
2 tsp caster sugar
2–3 tbsp whisky, or more
  to taste
200g (7oz) raspberries
sifted icing sugar, to dust

1 Put the oatmeal in a dry pan and toast over a moderate heat until golden brown. Tip into a bowl and leave to cool.

2 If using the raspberry jam, warm it with 4 tbsp water until melted, then strain through a sieve to make a jam sauce. This can be used to flavour the cream or dribbled through the cranachan. Set aside.

3 Whisk the cream, caster sugar, and whisky together until lightly whipped. Fold in the toasted oatmeal.

4 Divide half of the raspberries among four glasses. Spoon in a little of the jam sauce, if using. Half fill each glass with the cream mixture and sit most of the remaining raspberries on top. Spoon over more jam sauce, then finish with the rest of the cream mix. Smooth the top of each cranachan cream.

5 Garnish with the reserved raspberries and dust each pudding with icing sugar just before serving.

tip Instead of the jam sauce, you could use 1 tbsp crème de framboise liqueur.

This is a foolproof version of treacle tart — you cook it in a quiche dish, not a tin, so it will never leak, and you don't have the hassle of having to line the sides of the dish or tin with pastry.

LEMON AND TREACLE TART

serves 8–10

300g (10½oz) readymade
  shortcrust pastry
about 400g (14oz) golden syrup
150g (5½oz) fresh
  breadcrumbs
3 eggs, lightly beaten
grated zest and juice of
  2 lemons
clotted cream to serve

1 Preheat the oven to 180°C fan (200°C/gas 6). Butter a 35cm (14in) quiche dish.

2 Roll out the shortcrust pastry on a floured surface to 5mm (¼in) thick. Set the dish on the pastry as a template and cut around it. Place the disc of pastry in the bottom of the dish. Prick it all over with a fork, then bake for 10–12 minutes until lightly golden. Remove the dish from the oven and lower the temperature to 150°C fan (170°C/gas 3).

3 In a bowl, mix together the golden syrup, breadcrumbs, beaten eggs, and lemon zest and juice. Spoon into the quiche dish. Bake for 50 minutes to 1 hour until set and golden brown.

4 Allow to cool before serving warm with clotted cream.

Rosemary may seem an unusual herb to put with fruit, but it's great with pears and works with apples and bananas too. The humble crumble is a true British pudding — it's thought that it was first made during the Second World War, although probably not with butter.

PEAR AND ROSEMARY CRUMBLE WITH CINNAMON SAUCE

serves 6

sauce
600ml (1 pint) goat's milk
200g (7oz) caster sugar
100ml (3½fl oz) golden syrup
2 cinnamon sticks
1 tsp baking powder

filling
25g (scant 1oz) butter
10 pears, peeled, cored, and diced
6 tbsp golden syrup
1 sprig of fresh rosemary, broken into pieces

crumble
125g (4½oz) soft butter
350g (12oz) plain flour
150g (5½oz) Demerara sugar

illustrated on pages 134–135

1 First make the sauce by putting the milk, half of the sugar, and the golden syrup in a pan. Bring to the boil. Crumble the cinnamon sticks into the pan and add the baking powder and remaining sugar. Remove from the heat and stir well as the mix will rise quickly. Continue to whisk until it stops rising.

2 Return to the heat and bring back to the boil, whisking all the time. Turn down the heat and simmer for about 45 minutes, stirring frequently to prevent the sauce from catching and burning. When ready it should be a caramel colour, not burnt or black. Pass through a sieve into a clean pan. Set aside.

3 Preheat the oven to 200°C fan (220°C/gas 7).

4 Put the butter in a large non-stick pan and add the pears and 5 tbsp water. Bring to a simmer and cook for 8–10 minutes until the pears are soft but not broken down. Transfer the mixture to a large ovenproof dish about 2.5cm (1in) deep. Drizzle over the golden syrup and scatter on the rosemary.

5 To make the crumble topping, rub together the butter and flour in a bowl until the mixture resembles breadcrumbs. Add the sugar. Sprinkle the crumble evenly over the pears.

6 Bake for 40–45 minutes until golden brown. Remove the crumble from the oven and allow to cool slightly before serving with the warmed cinnamon sauce.

When I built my garden, the first thing I wanted in the
fruit tree patch was a mulberry. This fab fruit only has
a short season – and even shorter as the birds dive into
the berries too. Use them in this tart, or just warm them
in a little butter and sugar, then serve with vanilla ice
cream or clotted cream. Delicious.

UPSIDE-DOWN PEAR AND MULBERRY TART

serves 6–8

6 ripe Comice pears
350g (12oz) caster sugar
pared zest and juice of
  2 lemons
25g (scant 1oz) butter
375g (13oz) pre-rolled
  puff pastry
100g (3½oz) mulberries
  or blackberries
200ml (7fl oz) clotted cream
  to serve

1 Peel the pears, cut in half lengthways, and remove the core
with a teaspoon. Place the pears in a pan with 200g (7oz) of the
sugar and just enough water to cover. Add the lemon zest and
juice. Bring to the boil, then reduce the heat and gently simmer
for 15–25 minutes until tender (cooking time depends on the
ripeness of the pears) – test with a sharp knife. Remove from
the heat and leave the pears to cool in the syrup.

2 To make the caramel, put the remaining sugar into a 30cm
(12in) ovenproof frying or sauté pan and heat gently without
stirring until it melts and turns golden brown. Remove from
the heat, add the butter, and stir in gently until melted.

3 Preheat the oven to 200°C fan (220°C/gas 7).

4 Unfold the puff pastry on a lightly floured surface. Cut out a
circle slightly larger than the pan.

5 Drain the pears on kitchen paper, then arrange cut side up
in the caramel in the pan. Sprinkle with the mulberries. Cover
with the pastry and tuck the edges down inside the rim of the
pan. Bake for 20 minutes until the pastry is puffed and brown.

6 Remove the pan from the oven and leave to rest for 1 minute.
Then place an upturned plate on top of the pan and turn the
two over together so that the tart slips out onto the plate,
pastry on the base, pears on top. Serve with the clotted cream.

This is kind of like a treacle tart, and in fact it looks almost the same. But instead of breadcrumbs it uses ground almonds – and of course has no treacle in it. If you want to, you can add a little chocolate to the filling.

ALMOND TART

serves 4

375g (13oz) readymade sweet
   shortcrust pastry
4 eggs
250g (9oz) caster sugar
grated zest of 1 lemon
250g (9oz) ground almonds
55g (2oz) whole almonds,
   skin on
sifted icing sugar, to dust

1 Preheat the oven to 180°C fan (200°C/gas 6).

2 Roll out the pastry on a floured work surface and use to line a 23cm (9in) loose-bottomed tin. Prick the bottom of the pastry case all over with a fork. Set aside.

3 Beat the eggs and sugar together until creamy. Stir in the lemon zest and ground almonds.

4 Spoon the filling into the pastry case and scatter over the whole almonds. Bake for 45–50 minutes until the filling is golden brown and set.

5 Leave the tart to cool in the tin. When cold, transfer to a serving plate and dust with icing sugar to serve.

Wimpole Hall, Cambridgeshire

Wimpole Hall, one of the most important historic Georgian houses in the East of England, was the perfect place for this regional heat of The Great British Village Show. Despite the blustery weather, the village show spirit prevailed and the competition was tough. In the cakes and preserves tent, judges Lyn and Beryl had a tricky time choosing a winner from all the rich fruit cake entries. And a very competitive father and daughter went head to head in the flower arranging class.

These are great for breakfast and can also be served warm with a dollop of ice cream for a nice pudding. The secret is to get the custard to stay inside the Danish while they're cooking. That may need a bit of practice.

APRICOT, GINGER, AND CUSTARD DANISH

dough
650g (1lb 7oz) strong white
  bread flour
good pinch of salt
85g (3oz) caster sugar
20g (¾oz) fresh yeast
500g (1lb 2oz) chilled butter

filling and glaze
150g (5½oz) dried apricots,
  soaked to rehydrate and
  then chopped
270ml (9fl oz) thick apricot or
  plain yogurt
3 tbsp finely chopped
  stem ginger
1 can or carton thick custard
1 egg, beaten
2 tbsp apricot jam

1 To make the dough, place the flour, salt, and sugar in a large bowl. Cream the yeast with a little warm water and add to the flour. Mix together, gradually stirring in enough warm water to make a pliable dough.

2 Transfer the dough to a floured surface and knead for 5–10 minutes until smooth and elastic. Put the dough in an oiled bowl, cover, and allow to rest in the fridge for 1 hour.

3 Put the butter between two pieces of greaseproof paper and roll out to a rectangle about 1cm (½in) thick. Turn the chilled dough onto a floured work surface and roll out into a rectangle 60 x 30cm (24 x 12in). Turn the rectangle so it lies vertically in front of you. Place the butter over the bottom two-thirds of the dough rectangle. Fold the uncovered third of the dough down over the butter, then fold up the bottom third. Your dough will now be in three layers with butter in between. Return the dough to the fridge to chill for 1 hour.

4 Dust some more flour over the work surface and roll out the dough to the same sized rectangle as before. Repeat the folding process, one third on top of the other, then chill for another hour. Repeat the folding and chilling two more times, then leave the dough to rest in the fridge, wrapped in cling wrap, overnight if possible.

5 Line several baking trays with baking parchment. Roll out the dough to 3–5mm (⅛ – ¼in) thick and cut out as many 30 x 12cm (12 x 5in) rectangles as you can.

6 Put the dried apricots in a bowl and add the yogurt, ginger, and custard. Spoon some of this mixture down the middle of each of the dough rectangles, then fold them lengthways in half. Using a sharp knife, cut slashes about 10cm (4in) apart across the dough rectangles. Brush with the beaten egg and place on the baking trays. Leave to rise at room temperature for 1 hour.

7 Preheat the oven to 200°C fan (220°C/gas 7).

8 Bake the pastries for about 20 minutes until golden brown. Transfer to a wire rack to cool. When cooled, cut each pastry across into fingers.

9 Place the apricot jam in a small pan with a splash of water and heat gently until melted. Brush this onto the Danish pastries to glaze before serving.

Jean Gallimore was a stallholder at The Great British Village Show. This is her tried-and-tested variation of a friend's recipe, which she developed using redcurrants and strawberry jam.

JEAN GALLIMORE'S REDCURRANT FRANGIPAN

pastry
140g (5oz) plain flour
140g (5oz) self-raising flour
85g (3oz) caster sugar
140g (5oz) butter
1 egg
1 tbsp milk

filling
strawberry jam
115g (4oz) soft butter
85g (3oz) caster sugar
115g (4oz) ground almonds
2 eggs
85g (3oz) redcurrants

1 Preheat the oven to 150°C fan (170°C/gas 3).

2 To make the pastry, sift both flours together into a mixing bowl. Stir in the sugar. Rub in the butter until the mixture resembles fine breadcrumbs. Make a well in the centre and add the egg and milk. Knead to make a soft, smooth dough.

3 Cut out a sheet of greaseproof paper a little larger than a 23 x 33cm (9 x 13in) tin. Reserve some pastry for the trellis on top, then roll out the remaining pastry on the greaseproof paper. Lift into the tin to line it. (The paper makes it easy to lift the pastry.) Spread the strawberry jam over the pastry.

4 To make the filling, cream together the butter and sugar until light and fluffy. Gradually beat in the ground almonds and eggs. Spread the almond mixture over the jam and level.

5 Roll out the reserved pastry and cut into strips. Arrange over the filling in a trellis pattern. Place the redcurrants in the gaps of the trellis.

6 Bake for 30–40 minutes. Leave to cool in the tin.

I've no idea why this is called a roll as it's flat — a baked pudding of rich orange sponge, sliced apples, and apricot jam — but it tastes great.

HAMPSHIRE ROLL

serves 12

225g (8oz) soft unsalted butter
175g (6oz) caster sugar
3 eggs
2 tbsp double cream
finely grated zest of 1 orange
175g (6oz) plain flour, sifted
pinch of salt
675g (1½lb) apples
   (Cox or Granny Smith)
175g (6oz) apricot jam
sifted icing sugar

1 Preheat the oven to 180°C fan (200°C/gas 6). Use 55g (2oz) of the butter to generously grease a semi-circular tray mould (if you can find one), or a large pie dish.

2 To make the sponge, cream the sugar with the remaining butter until light, then beat in the eggs, double cream, and orange zest. Fold in the flour and salt.

3 Peel, core, and slice the apples. Spread 115g (4oz) of the jam over the bottom of the mould or dish. Sprinkle over half of the apples, then evenly spoon on half of the sponge mixture. Mix the remaining apples and jam together, place on top of the sponge in the mould, and cover with the remaining sponge. Smooth the top. Bake for 40–50 minutes until golden.

4 Serve sprinkled with icing sugar, and accompanied by clotted cream or hot custard.

At The Great British Village Show in Petworth, I visited a stall where a Yorkshire lady was selling Yorkshire curd tarts. They weren't there for long, as I bought the lot so my chefs could try them. Those tarts were the best I've tasted since going to Betty's tea room in York.

YORKSHIRE CURD TART

serves 10–12

500g (1lb 2oz) readymade
   shortcrust pastry
250g (9oz) soft unsalted butter
120g (4oz) caster sugar
500g (1lb 2oz) curd cheese
   (not cottage or cream cheese)
250g (9oz) seedless raisins
   or currants
2 heaped tbsp fresh wholemeal
   breadcrumbs
pinch of salt
½ tsp ground allspice or grated
   nutmeg, or to taste
4 eggs, well beaten

1 Preheat the oven to 200°C fan (220°C/gas 7).

2 Roll out the pastry on a lightly floured surface and use to line a 20–25cm (8–10in) loose-bottomed tart tin. Line the pastry case with foil and fill with baking beans. Bake blind for 10–15 minutes to set the base. Remove from the oven and remove the baking beans and foil.

3 While the pastry case is baking, cream the butter and sugar together until light. Mix in the curd cheese, raisins or currants, and breadcrumbs. Add the salt and spice and lastly the eggs.

4 Pour into the pastry case and bake for 30–35 minutes until golden brown and set. The pastry should be a nice brown.

tip   If you don't have baking beans, you can use uncooked rice or flour instead.

You have to thank James Birch for these cakes, because it was at his bakery in the village of Eccles in 1793 that these were first sold. Eccles cakes are now as popular in countries around the world as they are here in the UK.

ECCLES CAKES

makes 10

pastry
500g (1lb 2oz) readymade
    puff pastry
1 egg white to glaze
55g (2oz) Demerara sugar

filling
55g (2oz) butter
40g (1½oz) brown sugar
85g (3oz) currants
20g (¾oz) mixed peel
½ tsp ground allspice
½ tsp ground cinnamon

1 Preheat the oven to 180°C fan (200°C/gas 6).

2 Roll out the pastry on a lightly floured surface to make a large sheet about 3mm (⅛in) thick. Cut out 10 discs about 12cm (5in) in diameter. Place on a tray and leave to rest in the fridge while you make the filling.

3 Melt the butter and sugar together in a small pan. Allow to cool slightly, then stir in the remaining filling ingredients.

4 Place a large spoonful of filling in the centre of each of the pastry discs. Brush the pastry edges with a little egg white. To shape each cake, working around the circle, take a section of the pastry edge between your thumb and forefinger and fold it into the centre over the filling. Take the next section and fold it into the centre, overlapping the previous fold. Press down to seal. Continue until you have gathered up all the edges and have formed a neat round parcel.

5 Turn the parcel over and press down gently with the palm of your hand. Slash the pastry twice on the top with a sharp knife, brush with egg white, and sprinkle with Demerara sugar.

6 Place the cakes on a baking tray and bake for 20 minutes. Allow to cool before eating.

As a lad around Bonfire Night I remember having toffee in a wax bag. My gran used to put sultanas into the toffee as a way of getting my sis and me to eat fruit. This toffee tastes great, but check out the amount of sugar in it. It's no wonder I hated the dentist when I was young.

SULTANA AND TREACLE TOFFEE

450g (1lb) Demerara sugar
75g (2½oz) soft butter
½ tsp cream of tartar
100g (3½oz) black treacle
  or molasses
100g (3½oz) golden syrup
100g (3½oz) sultanas

1 Place the sugar and 150ml (5fl oz) water in a heavy saucepan and heat until all the sugar has dissolved.

2 Add the butter, cream of tartar, treacle, and golden syrup, and put a sugar thermometer in the pan. Bring to the boil, brushing the sides of the pan down with a pastry brush dipped in water to stop crystals forming. Do not stir.

3 When the mixture reaches 115°C (the soft-ball stage), remove from the heat and add the sultanas. Stir to mix.

4 Pour into an 18cm (7½in) round or square tin and allow to cool. When set, break into pieces and store in a jar.

4

cakes and biscuits

Victoria Sponge Cake **Chocolate Sponge Cake** Maureen Williams's Rich Fruit Cake **Honey Cake** Cherry Cake **Betty Gilbert's Lemon Cake** Margaret Edge's Toffee Apple Cake or Pudding **Orange Pound Cake** Chocolate Stout Cake **Marian Brewer's Chocolate and Banana Cake** Anne Ashley's Parkin **Carrot Cake** Fran Wright's Whisky Mac **Chocolate and Ginger Flapjacks** Sticky Gingerbread

I once entered a WI competition for a laugh, to see how I would do. Bloody hopeless. You were judged on ten points and I got disqualified on nine of them — the wrong sugar, the wrong jam, and so on. So don't use this cake in any competitions. It tastes great though.

VICTORIA SPONGE CAKE

serves 10–12

5 eggs
140g (5oz) caster sugar
140g (5oz) sifted plain flour
pinch of salt
about 6 tbsp raspberry jam
250–300ml (9–10fl oz) double
  cream, whipped
sifted icing sugar, to dust

1 Preheat the oven to 190°C fan (210°C/gas 6½). Grease and flour a 20cm (8in) cake tin.

2 Whisk the eggs and caster sugar together using an electric mixer until pale, fluffy, and thickened. Fold in the flour and salt. When combined, pour into the prepared cake tin.

3 Bake for 20–25 minutes until well risen and golden brown, and springy to the touch. Allow to cool slightly, then turn out onto a wire rack to cool completely.

4 Cut the cake horizontally in half. Spread the raspberry jam over the "cut" side of the base, then top with whipped cream. Set the top of the cake gently on the cream. Dust with icing sugar before serving.

tip If the cake mixture appears curdled at any stage, stir in 1 tbsp flour to bring it back together, then gradually fold in the rest of the flour.

You can't beat a good chocolate cake, and this is really good. The problem is that it's like opening a packet of chocolate digestives — you have to eat the whole lot, even though you only really wanted one.

CHOCOLATE SPONGE CAKE

serves 10–12

cake
5 eggs
225g (8oz) caster sugar
160g (5½oz) self-raising flour
3 tbsp cocoa powder
85g (3oz) unsalted butter, melted
about 6 tbsp jam of your choice (raspberry, strawberry, or blackcurrant)
sifted icing sugar or cocoa powder, to dust

cream
250–300ml (9–10fl oz) double cream
2–3 tbsp icing sugar, sifted
1 vanilla pod, split open and seeds scraped out, or dash of pure vanilla extract

1 Preheat the oven to 190°C fan (210°C/gas 6½). Grease and flour a 20cm (8in) cake tin.

2 Whisk the eggs and caster sugar together using an electric mixer until pale, fluffy, and thickened. Sift the flour and cocoa powder together, then fold into the egg mixture. When combined, gently stir in the melted butter.

3 Pour into the prepared cake tin. Bake for 25–30 minutes until well risen and springy to the touch. Leave to cool slightly, then turn out onto a wire rack to cool completely.

4 Whip the cream with the icing sugar and vanilla seeds or extract until thick and fluffy.

5 Cut the cake horizontally in half. Spread the jam over the bottom cake layer and top with the whipped cream. Set the top of the cake on the cream. Dust with icing sugar or cocoa powder before serving.

tip Use a balloon whisk to gently fold the flour into the egg and sugar mixture, to avoid any flour "pockets".

Maureen Williams won the rich fruit cake class at Dyffryn Gardens. She says, "This is full of fruit, nuts, and cherries and has plenty of booze in it too. The cake is at its best when it has matured for 4–6 weeks, but it will keep well for a year or more".

MAUREEN WILLIAMS'S RICH FRUIT CAKE

250g (9oz) sultanas
250g (9oz) raisins
250g (9oz) currants
55g (2oz) mixed peel
125g (4½oz) glacé cherries, quartered
4 tbsp rum
grated zest of 1 orange and 1 lemon
75g (2½oz) flaked almonds
225g (8oz) soft butter
225g (8oz) light soft brown sugar
4 extra large free-range eggs, at room temperature, beaten
75g (2½oz) ground almonds
225g (8oz) plain flour
¾ tsp mixed spice
3 tbsp brandy

tip If you intend to eat the cake within a week, wrap it in cling film. If you are going to leave the cake to mature, wrap it in greaseproof paper and foil.

1 The day before, mix the dried fruits, mixed peel, cherries, and rum in a bowl. Cover and leave to soak for at least 12 hours.

2 Preheat the oven to 150°C fan (170°C/gas 3). Double line a 20cm (8in) round cake tin with greaseproof paper and tie four or five bands of brown paper around the outside of the tin.

3 Add the zests and flaked almonds to the fruit mixture.

4 Cream the butter with the sugar until soft. Gradually beat in the eggs. Fold in the ground almonds. Sift the flour with the spice and fold in, followed by the fruit mixture.

5 Spoon the mixture into the tin and level the top. Cover with a double square of greaseproof paper with a hole/vent cut in the middle about the size of a 50p piece. Place the cake in the oven on one shelf below the middle, with four or five layers of brown paper underneath the tin. Bake for 30 minutes, then continue baking as follows: 130°C fan (150°C/gas 2) for 45 minutes; 120°C fan (140°C/gas 1) for 1½ hours; and finally, 110°C fan (130°C/gas ½) for up to 2 hours. These times may vary depending on your oven, so check the cake after 4–4½ hours' baking and remove when cooked.

6 Place the tin on a wire rack and remove the top paper and brown paper. Leave to cool for 30–45 minutes before turning the cake out of the tin. After the cake has cooled for about 2½ hours, and whilst still warm, spoon 4 tsp of brandy over the top. Cover and leave overnight to cool completely. Then turn the cake upside down and spoon the remaining brandy over it.

The rich fruit cake class is always one of the most popular, but there are very strict rules on presentation to follow if you want to be in with a chance. The cake must not be made using cake liners. It must be 8 inches untrimmed, round or square, and be displayed on a board. Judges are also looking for a fine texture and well-balanced flavour.

THE RICH FRUIT CAKE CLASS

Judge Lyn Blackburn
"Always use good quality butter, never cheap margarine or spreads. Do not use old spices; buy them often and in small amounts."

Judge Beryl Village
"Make the cake to your own preference. Get the balance correct by putting in the fruit you especially like. To make a nice change, try using prunes, chopped apricots, and chopped pineapple."

Judge Lyn Blackburn
"To keep the surface of the cake flat and smooth and to prevent any fruit popping up, take a saucer of cold water, dip the back of four fingers into the water and glide over the surface of the cake before cooking. Repeat until the whole of the top has been done."

Judge Beryl Village
"For baking, brush a round of greaseproof paper with butter and lay it on top of the cake. To protect the sides from burning, wrap the cake with brown baking paper."

Try this for afternoon tea. The great thing about making cakes with honey, as well as with syrups, is that it keeps them so wonderfully moist.

HONEY CAKE

serves 8

175g (6oz) clear honey
150g (5oz) butter
80g (3oz) light muscovado
  sugar
2 eggs, beaten
200g (7oz) self-raising flour,
  sifted

icing
55g (2oz) icing sugar, sifted
1 tbsp clear honey

1 Preheat the oven to 180°C fan (200°C/gas 6). Butter an 18cm (7in) cake tin and line the bottom with greaseproof paper.

2 Put the honey, butter, and sugar into a large pan. Add 1 tbsp water and heat gently until melted. Remove from the heat and transfer to a bowl. Mix in the eggs and flour.

3 Spoon into the cake tin and bake for 40–45 minutes until the cake is springy to the touch and shrinking a little from the sides of the tin. Cool slightly in the tin before turning out onto a wire rack.

4 While the cake is still warm, make the icing by mixing the sugar and honey together with 2–3 tsp hot water. Spoon this over the cake and serve.

Talking to the ladies at the WI stalls, I learned that cherry cake is one of the most popular cakes they sell. I tried three of them. For me, cherry cake brings back memories of my gran and auntie. They were both brilliant at baking and this recipe is one of theirs.

CHERRY CAKE

serves 10–12

225g (8oz) soft butter
225g (8oz) golden caster sugar
4 large eggs, lightly beaten
225g (8oz) plain flour
½ tsp baking powder
250g (9oz) glacé cherries, quartered (no need to rinse)
110g (4oz) ground almonds
few drops of almond or vanilla extract
1 tbsp milk
2 tbsp Demerara sugar

1 Preheat the oven to 180°C fan (200°C/gas 6). Grease a 20cm (8in) cake tin that is 10cm (4in) deep and line the bottom with baking parchment.

2 Cream the butter and caster sugar together until light, pale, and fluffy. Gradually beat in the eggs, a little at a time. Sift the flour and baking powder together, then carefully fold into the creamed mixture using a large metal spoon. Add the quartered cherries and ground almonds, and carefully fold these into the mixture, adding the almond extract and milk.

3 Spoon into the prepared tin and level the top with the back of the spoon. Sprinkle with the Demerara sugar.

4 Bake in the centre of the oven for 1 hour. Cover with foil and continue baking for 30 minutes until the cake has shrunk away from the side of the tin and the centre is springy to the touch.

5 Cool the cake in the tin for 15 minutes before turning it out onto a wire rack to cool completely. Store in an airtight container for up to 5 days.

Betty Gilbert ran a stall at The Great British Village Show. She says, "When I joined Lichfield WI Markets in the 1980s, our lemon cakes always had customers queuing. I normally make 21–24 cakes, and even then they sell out in the first couple of hours".

BETTY GILBERT'S LEMON CAKE

175g (6oz) soft margarine
175g (6oz) caster sugar
grated zest and juice of
  1 large lemon
2 large eggs, beaten
175g (6oz) self-raising flour
4 tbsp milk
2 tbsp granulated sugar

1 Preheat the oven to 180°C/gas 4.

2 Lightly grease a 900g (2lb) loaf tin or two 450g (1lb) tins and line the bottom with greaseproof paper.

3 Cream the margarine with the caster sugar and lemon zest until light and creamy (by adding lemon zest at this stage more flavour is released). Beat in the eggs. Fold in the flour, then add the milk.

4 Spoon the mixture into the tin(s) and level the top. Bake for 30–35 minutes until firm to the touch.

5 Meanwhile, add the granulated sugar to the lemon juice and heat until almost completely dissolved.

6 When the cake is baked and whilst still hot, prick the surface lightly and brush on the lemon juice mix. Allow to cool before removing from the tin.

Margaret Edge was a stallholder at The Great British Village Show and this is her Toffee Apple Cake recipe. She says, "Almonds have been used but other nuts are just as good. The cake is delicious served warm with cream, custard, or ice cream".

MARGARET EDGE'S TOFFEE APPLE CAKE OR PUDDING

175g (6oz) soft unsalted butter or margarine
175g (6oz) light muscovado sugar
3 large eggs, beaten
175g (6oz) self-raising flour
1 tsp mixed spice
3 medium apples (either dessert or cooking – Bramleys are excellent), peeled, cored, and sliced
30g (1oz) flaked almonds
1 tbsp Demerara sugar

1 Preheat the oven to 160°C fan (180°C/gas 4). Grease and line a 20cm (8in) tin.

2 Cream the butter with the muscovado sugar until fluffy. Beat in the eggs. Sift the flour and mixed spice together and fold into the creamed mixture.

3 Spread half the mixture into the tin. Cover with two-thirds of the apple slices. Spread the rest of the mixture over the apples, and arrange the rest of the apples on top. Sprinkle over the flaked almonds and then the Demerara sugar.

4 Bake in the middle of the oven for about 45 minutes until a skewer comes out clean. Serve warm or cool before serving.

I collect cookbooks from the eighteenth and nineteenth centuries, and while flicking through them I found quite a few orange or lemon cakes. This recipe is a modern version of one of them.

ORANGE POUND CAKE

serves 6–8

cake
125g (4½oz) soft, lightly salted butter
125g (4½oz) vanilla caster sugar
125g (4½oz) self-raising flour sifted with 1 tsp baking powder
grated zest of 1 large orange
juice of ½ large orange
125g (4½oz) eggs (about 2 medium eggs)
1 rounded tbsp ground almonds (optional)

butter cream
125g (4½oz) granulated sugar
3 tbsp orange juice
2 egg yolks, beaten
125g (4½oz) soft, lightly salted butter

to finish
handful of flaked almonds
sifted icing sugar

1 Preheat the oven to 150°C fan (170°C/gas 3). Line the bottom and long sides of a 23cm (9in) loaf tin with baking parchment – cut the piece of parchment 23cm (9in) wide and long enough to go down one long side, across the bottom, and up the other long side. There is no need to grease or line the short ends of the tin.

2 Put all the ingredients for the cake into a bowl and mix until smooth. Spoon the mixture into the loaf tin. Bake for 40–45 minutes until golden brown and springy to touch. A skewer inserted in the centre should come out clean.

3 Leave the cake to cool in the tin for about 15 minutes, then take hold of the edges of the baking parchment and lift the cake onto a wire rack. Leave to cool.

4 To make the butter cream, dissolve the sugar with the juice, then put a sugar thermometer in the pan and boil to 115°C, or a fraction higher. Put the egg yolks in a bowl. Tip in the boiling syrup and beat vigorously with an electric mixer. Before the mixture is cold, add the soft butter and beat again until light, creamy, and thickened. Chill in the fridge to firm up.

5 Cut the cake horizontally in half. Fill with the butter cream, keeping back a little to smooth on the top. Scatter over the almonds and dust with icing sugar before serving.

tip To make vanilla sugar quickly, place the sugar in a bowl and stir in the sticky seeds scraped from a split vanilla pod.

Moist is the word for this cake, and it's full of flavour. Don't even think of making this with lager. It must be made with a rich, dark stout.

CHOCOLATE STOUT CAKE

serves 10–12

cake
115g (4oz) very soft butter
280g (10oz) dark soft
  brown sugar
2 large eggs, beaten
55g (2oz) cocoa powder
200ml (7fl oz) stout
175g (6oz) plain flour
¼ tsp baking powder
1 tbsp bicarbonate of soda

icing
115g (4oz) icing sugar, sifted
55g (2oz) very soft butter
2 tbsp stout
115g (4oz) dark chocolate
  (50–55% cocoa solids)
30g (1oz) walnut pieces,
  finely chopped

to decorate
8 walnut halves
cocoa powder

1 Preheat the oven to 180°C fan (200°C/gas 6). Lightly grease two 20cm (8in) cake tins that are 4cm (1½in) deep, and line the bottoms with baking parchment.

2 Cream the butter and sugar together, beating thoroughly for 3–4 minutes until pale and fluffy. Gradually beat in the eggs, beating well between each addition.

3 Put the cocoa powder in a small bowl and gradually stir in the stout until the mixture is smooth.

4 Sift the flour, baking powder, and bicarbonate of soda into the bowl. Carefully and lightly fold in, gradually adding the cocoa and stout mixture at the same time. Divide the cake mixture equally between the two tins.

5 Bake in the centre of the oven for 30–35 minutes. The cakes should be flat on top and feel springy, and will have shrunk slightly from the side of the tins. Leave them to cool in the tins for 5 minutes before turning out onto a wire rack to cool further, carefully removing the lining paper.

6 To make the icing, beat the icing sugar and butter together until blended, then gradually add the stout, making sure it is thoroughly mixed in after each addition.

7 Melt the chocolate in a bowl set over a pan of hot water (the base of the bowl should not touch the water). Allow to cool slightly, then mix into the icing.

8 Remove one-third of the icing to a separate bowl and stir in the chopped walnuts. Leave the two batches of icing to cool to a spreadable consistency.

9 Sandwich the cakes together with the walnut icing. Spread the remaining plain icing on top of the cake, using a palette knife. Dust the walnut halves with cocoa powder, then arrange them on top of the cake. Try to be patient and allow the icing to become firm before eating!

The Great British Village Show
Dyffryn Gardens, Wales

On a beautiful Welsh summer's day, the Great British Village Show took place at the spectacular Grade 1 listed gardens on the outskirts of Cardiff. Enthusiastic exhibitors arrived laden with vegetables they hoped would be the heaviest on the scales, flowers they hoped would make up the winning arrangements, and cakes and preserves they hoped would be the tastiest on the showbench. In the marrow class, two brothers – Welsh record holders – took the red rosette with "the Crocodile Dundee of Cardiff" which weighed a whopping 101lb 6oz, the same as an average teenager!

Marian Brewer was a stallholder at The Great British Village Show. She says, "I always use vegetarian margarine as I find it lighter than other margarines or butter. My daughter says this is delicious warmed for 30 seconds in the microwave, and served with ice cream".

MARIAN BREWER'S CHOCOLATE AND BANANA CAKE

225g (8oz) caster sugar
225g (8oz) vegetarian soft margarine
225g (8oz) self-raising flour
3–4 large eggs
2 heaped tbsp chocolate powder
1 dessertspoon treacle
2 ripe bananas

to decorate (optional)
vegetarian soft margarine
sifted icing sugar
chocolate powder
banana chips
chocolate shapes

1 Preheat the oven to 150°C fan (170°C/gas 3). Grease a 20cm (8in) square tin and line with baking parchment.

2 Put the sugar and margarine in a bowl and beat with an electric mixer until creamy. Gradually beat in the flour and eggs to make a light, smooth, creamy mixture. Add the chocolate powder, treacle, and one and a half bananas, and continue beating until smooth.

3 Pour the mixture into the tin. Chop the rest of the banana into the cake and gently mix in.

4 Bake for about 45 minutes until firm. Cooking time may vary, according to your oven, and also if you are cooking other items in the oven at the same time. Allow to cool in the tin.

5 To decorate, make some butter cream with soft margarine, icing sugar, and chocolate powder, mixing to the consistency of double cream. Make a piping bag from greaseproof paper and fill with the chocolate cream, then pipe scrolls on the top of the cake, from the middle out to the edge. Place banana chips and chocolate shapes into the swirls.

Anne Ashley ran a stall at The Great British Village Show. She says, "A friend gave me this recipe. It's one of her mother's. It contains no egg, so is good for people who are allergic or intolerant to egg".

ANNE ASHLEY'S PARKIN

450g (1lb) golden syrup, or
   350g (12oz) golden syrup and
   100g (4oz) black treacle
225g (8oz) butter or margarine
½ pint mug mixed milk
   and water
½ pint mug plain flour
½ pint mug self-raising
   flour
½ pint mug medium
   oatmeal
2 rounded tsp ground ginger
1 tsp bicarbonate of soda

1 Preheat the oven to 150°C fan (150°C/gas 3). Line a 22cm (9in) square tin with baking parchment.

2 Gently melt the syrup, or syrup and treacle, with the butter or margarine. Remove from the heat.

3 Warm the milk and water.

4 In a large bowl, mix together the flours, oatmeal, and ginger. Pour the syrup mix onto the dry ingredients and mix well. Stir the bi-carb into the warm milk and water mix, then pour into the bowl and beat until well incorporated.

5 Pour the mixture into the tin and bake for 35–40 minutes until firm and springy. Cool in the tin.

6 Keep in an airtight container until the parkin starts to go sticky on top.

Good fresh carrots are a must for this recipe. I know it sounds daft, but compare a fresh carrot just pulled from the ground with one that's been wrapped in a bag on a supermarket shelf after a journey from some far-flung country. You'll see what I mean.

CARROT CAKE

serves 12–14

cake
5 medium carrots, scraped
  and sliced
juice of 2 oranges
125ml (4fl oz) corn oil
4 eggs, separated
375g (13oz) caster sugar
350g (12oz) "00" pasta flour
  or plain flour
15g (½oz) baking powder

topping
250g (9oz) mascarpone or good
  cream cheese
250ml (9fl oz) double cream
2 tbsp caster sugar
2–3 tbsp Cointreau, to taste

1 Preheat the oven to 180°C fan (200°C/gas 6). Butter a 30cm (12in) springform cake tin and line the bottom of the tin with a disc of greaseproof paper.

2 To make the cake, place the carrots in a pan, cover with water, and add the orange juice. Bring to the boil and cook until tender. Drain and cool. Put the carrots in a blender with the corn oil and the egg yolks, and blitz to a purée.

3 Transfer the carrot purée to a bowl and fold in the sugar, flour, and baking powder, mixing well together. Whisk the egg whites until stiff and gently fold in.

4 Pour the mixture into the prepared tin and bake for 30–35 minutes until golden brown and springy to the touch, and a skewer inserted in the centre comes out clean.

5 Cool in the tin for a few minutes, then turn out onto a wire rack to cool completely.

6 To make the topping, whisk together the mascarpone, cream, and sugar in a bowl. Stir in Cointreau to taste. Spread the topping over the cake. Chill to set the topping before serving, if you like.

Fran Wright ran a stall at The Great British Village Show. For a non-alcoholic version of her Whisky Mac recipe — which she calls Apple Jack cake — follow exactly the same recipe, but omit the whisky and ginger wine and replace them with 85ml (3fl oz) of apple juice.

FRAN WRIGHT'S WHISKY MAC

450g (1lb) dried mixed fruit
115g (4oz) margarine
175g (6oz) Demerara sugar
1 tsp bicarbonate of soda
2 eggs
115g (4oz) self-raising flour
115g (4oz) plain flour
2 tbsp whisky
4 tbsp ginger wine

1 Preheat the oven to 120°C fan (140°C/gas 1). Line two 450g (1lb) loaf tins with liners or baking parchment.

2 Combine the mixed fruit, margarine, Demerara sugar, bicarbonate of soda, and 175ml (6fl oz) water in a saucepan. Bring to the boil and boil for 2 minutes, then remove from the heat and leave to cool.

3 Put the contents of the saucepan into a mixing bowl. Stir in the eggs and then the flours, followed by the whisky and ginger wine. Mix well.

4 Divide the mixture between the tins. Place in the preheated oven and bake for 1 hour, turning the tins round halfway through so that they cook evenly. Test with a skewer to make sure they are cooked in the centre. Remove from the oven and leave to cool in the tins.

In northern parts of the UK I've heard this called nutty flip. Whatever name you use, flapjacks are best baked in advance. The syrup makes them even stickier when they are left for a few days.

CHOCOLATE AND GINGER FLAPJACKS

makes 8 flapjacks

200g (7oz) soft brown sugar
200g (7oz) butter
2 tbsp golden syrup
350g (12oz) porridge oats
3 tbsp chopped stem ginger
   in syrup
100g (3½oz) chocolate chips

1 Preheat the oven to 150°C fan (170°C/gas 3). Lightly grease a 30 x 20 x 5cm (12 x 8 x 2in) tin and line the bottom with baking parchment or greaseproof paper.

2 Place the sugar, butter, and golden syrup in a saucepan and heat gently until the butter has melted, stirring occasionally. Take the saucepan off the heat and stir in the oats, ginger, and chocolate chips, mixing thoroughly.

3 Pour the mixture into the tin and press it out evenly using the back of a spoon. Bake in the centre of the oven for 40–45 minutes. Allow to cool in the tin for 10 minutes before cutting into oblong bars. Leave the flapjacks in the tin until quite cold before removing them.

This won't last long. The texture is similar to that of toffee pudding, really moist. It's great on its own or with a dollop of ice cream. The stem ginger and syrup are what make it so sticky.

STICKY GINGERBREAD

serves 6

140g (5oz) stem ginger in
   syrup (8 pieces)
175g (6oz) self-raising flour
1 tsp ground ginger
½ tsp ground cinnamon
½ tsp ground cloves
1 tsp baking powder
1 tsp bicarbonate of soda
2 eggs
75g (2½oz) soft butter
115g (4oz) molasses sugar
1 tbsp black treacle
   or molasses
1 heaped tsp freshly grated
   fresh ginger
175g (6oz) peeled and cored
   Bramley apples,
   chopped small

1 Preheat the oven to 180°C fan (200°C/gas 6). Generously butter six 175ml (6fl oz) individual pudding basins.

2 Put the pieces of stem ginger in a food processor and blitz for 7–10 seconds to chop small. Take care not to purée the ginger. Set aside.

3 Sift the flour, spices, baking powder, and bicarbonate of soda into a mixing bowl. Add the eggs, butter, sugar, treacle, and fresh ginger. Using an electric mixer, whisk together, gradually adding 150–175ml (5–6fl oz) warm water to make a smooth mixture. Fold in the apples and stem ginger.

4 Divide the mixture among the buttered pudding basins, filling them three-quarters full. Set them on a baking sheet and bake in the centre of the oven for 35 minutes until they feel firm and springy to the touch.

5 Remove them from the oven and let them stand for about 5 minutes, then run a small palette knife around the edges of the basins and turn out the gingerbreads. Allow them to get completely cold and keep them wrapped in cling film or in an airtight tin for up to 5 days.

tip Use a greased spoon to measure the treacle, and push it into the bowl with the help of a spatula or another spoon.

5

savoury breads and pickles

Lincolnshire Poacher Scones **Mustard Pickle** Cauliflower Piccalilli

Cold-Pickled Shallots and Garlic with Herbs Oatcakes **Fennel**

and Saffron Flowerpot Bread Beetroot and Chive Breads **Pumpkin**

and Marjoram Bread

Without doubt, we produce some of the best cheese here in the UK. Lincolnshire Poacher, made by Simon Jones on his dairy farm in — you guessed it — Lincolnshire, is one I particularly like.

LINCOLNSHIRE POACHER SCONES

makes 20–24 scones

675g (1½lb) plain flour
40g (1½oz) baking powder
1 tsp salt
140g (5oz) butter
200g (7oz) Lincolnshire
  Poacher cheese, grated
3 eggs, beaten
200ml (7fl oz) milk
beaten egg to glaze

1 Preheat the oven to 180°C fan (200°C/gas 6).

2 Sift the flour, baking powder, and salt into a large bowl. Add the butter and rub together. Add 140g (5oz) of the grated cheese followed by the eggs and milk. Combine quickly to make a ball of dough.

3 On a floured surface, gently roll out the dough to 2.5–4cm (1–1½in) thick. Using a 6cm (2½in) pastry cutter, cut out rounds. Arrange the scones on a greased baking tray.

4 Brush the scones with beaten egg and sprinkle the rest of the cheese on top. Bake for 20–25 minutes until golden. Serve the scones warm or cool.

tip Re-roll any dough trimmings, so you can cut out more scones.

It doesn't take much to please me — a pork pie, some pickled shallots, and this pickle, and I'm a happy man.

MUSTARD PICKLE

fills about 2 large kilner jars

225g (8oz) table salt
450g (1lb) baby onions or
    shallots, peeled
225g (8oz) cherry tomatoes
450g (1lb) cauliflower florets
450g (1lb) cucumber, deseeded
    and cut into large dice
1 tbsp capers
125g (4½oz) butter
25g (scant 1oz) plain flour
500ml (17fl oz) malt vinegar
115g (4oz) caster sugar
1 tbsp turmeric
2½ tsp mustard powder
black pepper

1 Dissolve the salt in about 4 litres (7 pints) of water. Put the onions or quartered shallots, tomatoes, and cauliflower in a large bowl and cover with the salted water. Cover with cling film and keep in the fridge or a cool place for 24 hours.

2 Drain the vegetables in a colander and tip them into a large pan. Add the diced cucumber and capers and cover with 2 litres (3½ pints) of fresh water. Bring to the boil and boil for 10 minutes. Drain again and put the vegetables in a bowl.

3 Melt the butter in a saucepan, then add the flour and stir well to make a roux. Slowly add the vinegar, stirring all the time. Cook for a few minutes until thickened. Add the sugar, turmeric, and mustard powder, and season with pepper. Pour over the vegetables and stir to mix. Pack the vegetables into sterilized jars and seal.

4 Leave in the fridge for at least 5 days before eating so that the vegetables can absorb all the mustardy flavours. The pickle can be kept in the fridge for up to 2 weeks.

tip   Sterilize the jars with boiling water, or by heating them in a hot oven for about 4 minutes.

For a piccalilli, I like the pieces of veg to be chunky and not too small. This cauliflower piccalilli is what you need with pork pies and cold meats.

CAULIFLOWER PICCALILLI

makes about 1kg (2¼lb)

325ml (11fl oz) white
 wine vinegar
175ml (6fl oz) malt vinegar
175g (6oz) caster sugar
25g (scant 1oz) mustard
 powder
20g (¾oz) turmeric
4 tsp cornflour
1 small cauliflower, cut into
 1cm (½in) dice
1 small onion, cut into 1cm
 (½in) dice
½ cucumber, peeled, deseeded,
 and cut into 1cm (½in) dice
pinch of salt

1 Put both of the vinegars in a pan and bring to the boil, then remove from the heat and allow to cool.

2 Mix the sugar, mustard, turmeric, and cornflour together in another pan. Pour in half of the cooled vinegar and mix well, then add the remainder of the vinegar and cook for about 2–3 minutes, stirring. Leave to cool.

3 Place the diced cauliflower, onion, and cucumber in a bowl. Season with salt. Pour over the cooled vinegar mixture and stir to mix. Transfer the piccalilli to a sterilized jar and seal. Store in the fridge for up to a week.

A lot of work goes into growing shallots for the village shows — some people grow 250 to get just nine to exhibit. Apparently the perfect shallot has to fit inside the judge's 3cm (1¼in) ring.

COLD-PICKLED SHALLOTS AND GARLIC WITH HERBS

fills 1 kilner jar

250g (9oz) salt
2 litres (3½ pints) water
800g (1¾lb) shallots
2 bulbs garlic, broken into
  cloves
4 sprigs of fresh rosemary
4 sprigs of fresh thyme
600ml (1 pint) malt vinegar

1 Mix half the salt with half of the water in a bowl. Add the shallots and garlic and leave in a cool place overnight.

2 Drain and peel them. Make up another batch of brine in the bowl with the remaining salt and water. Add the onions and garlic and leave in this mixture for about 72 hours (3 days), covered and in the fridge.

3 Drain again and pack into a sterilized jar with the herbs. Pour over the vinegar. Cover and seal, then leave for 3 months in the fridge before eating. The pickle can be kept for up to 3 months in the fridge.

Variation Hot-pickled shallots and garlic with herbs

Put the shallots and garlic in a saucepan of water and bring to the boil. Boil for 3–4 minutes. Drain and peel, then place on a tray. Dust all over with 100g (3½oz) table salt and set aside for a day. Rinse well, then cook in 800ml (1⅓ pints) malt vinegar with the herbs for 8 minutes. Pack the shallots, garlic, and herbs into a sterilized jar and pour in the hot vinegar. Cover and seal, then leave for 3 weeks before eating.

The pickling shallots had a maximum points value of 15, which was broken down into five categories:
Condition 5 points
Uniformity 4 points
Shape 2 points
Size 2 points
Colour 2 points

At The Great British Village Show the requirement for this class was a dish of 9 pickling shallots. Each shallot had to pass through a 30mm (1¼ inch) ring in order to qualify.

THE PICKLING SHALLOTS CLASS

Head Judge Medwyn Williams

"When selecting shallots for competition, use a National Vegetable Society approved ring to ensure bulbs are within the size tolerance. Also check for uniformity. You should ensure that bulbs are sound, with unbroken skins. Where tied, natural raffia should be used."

Judge Gerald Treweek

"To grow shallots for competition, pick out your smallest and pot them into a medium container with very little feed. Sit the pots on a bed with very little feed and water the bottom of the pots."

Judge John Trim

"Top exhibition variety, and virtually unbeatable on the showbench, is Hative de Niort. However, there are a few challengers coming along: Jermore is winning prizes, as is Aristocrat. In the kitchen, the top choice for chefs is Jermore." (See pages 216–217 for more information on varieties.)

There are two types of oatcake in the UK. One is Scottish and the other, which is more like a pancake, is made in north Staffordshire. I make loads of Scottish oatcakes, as I love them with cheese and they keep so well.

OATCAKES

makes 16 oatcakes

125g (4½oz) medium oatmeal
125g (4½oz) plain flour
60g (2oz) lard, dripping, or
  poultry fat
1 tsp salt

glaze
1 egg
1 tbsp milk
1 tsp caster sugar

1 Preheat the oven to 180°C fan (200°C/gas 6).

2 Mix the oatmeal and flour in a bowl. Rub in the fat, then add the salt. Mix in enough cold water – about 3½tbsp – to make a soft but not tacky dough.

3 Roll out on an oatmeal-strewn board. Cut out circles with a 6cm (2½in) pastry cutter. If you like your oatcakes really thin, slap them out between your oatmealy hands (this is tricky as the edges begin to crack, but it's the old Welsh method and it does produce very good oatcakes). Alternatively, cut out four dinner-plate rounds and quarter them.

4 Make the glaze by lightly beating the egg with the milk and caster sugar.

5 Place the oatcakes on a non-stick baking tray, brush with the glaze, and bake for 15–20 minutes until golden brown and cooked through. Alternatively, cook on an ungreased griddle over a moderate heat for 2–3 minutes on each side.

6 Store in an airtight box. If you like, toast lightly before the fire to warm through before serving.

As you've probably guessed, I'm not just a lover of food, I like my garden and my vegetables too. This recipe gives me the best of both worlds. You will need eight small terracotta flowerpots (250ml/8fl oz in volume).

FENNEL AND SAFFRON FLOWERPOT BREAD

makes 8 breads

dough
1½ tsp salt
60g (2oz) soft butter
500g (1lb 2oz) strong white
   bread flour
20g (¾oz) fresh yeast

flavouring
1 tbsp olive oil
1 red onion, chopped or sliced
½ fennel bulb, thinly sliced
2 tbsp fennel seeds, toasted
pinch of saffron threads
splash of white wine
2–4 tbsp chopped fresh dill

1 Place the salt, butter, and flour in a large bowl and rub together. Put the yeast in a small bowl and cream with a little warm water, then add to the flour mixture. Mix together, adding enough warm water to make a dough.

2 Turn the dough out onto a lightly floured surface and knead for 5 minutes until smooth and elastic. Shape into a ball, place in a clean oiled bowl, and cover with a damp cloth. Leave in a warm place for about 1 hour until well risen.

3 Meanwhile, heat the oil in a non-stick frying pan and sauté the red onion for 1–2 minutes to soften. Add the fennel slices and half the fennel seeds, and continue to sauté for a few minutes. Transfer to a bowl.

4 Mix the saffron with the wine. Add to the onion and fennel, together with the dill and stir together. Leave to cool.

5 Line the inside of each flowerpot with a piece of baking parchment. Add the saffron mixture to the dough and mix well. Divide the dough into eight pieces, shape each into a ball, and place in the flowerpots. Cover with a damp cloth and leave in a warm place for about 1 hour until risen to the top of the pots.

6 Preheat the oven to 200°C fan (220°C/gas 7).

7 Sprinkle the breads with the remaining toasted fennel seeds, then bake for 30–35 minutes until risen and golden brown. Remove the breads from the oven and turn out onto a wire rack. Allow to cool before serving.

illustrated on pages 186–187

People either love beetroot or hate it. I love it. It tastes so good in salads and with cold meats. This is a recipe I made up to use a crop of beets from my garden. The breads not only look great but taste brill. Try splitting them and putting a slice of cold pork or beef inside.

BEETROOT AND CHIVE BREADS

makes 4 breads

20g (¾oz) fresh yeast
500g (1lb 2oz) strong white
  bread flour
1½ tsp salt
25g (scant 1oz) fresh chives,
  chopped
150–200g (5–7oz) cooked
  beetroot, diced

1 Cream the yeast with a little warm water. Put the flour and salt in a large bowl and add the yeast. Mix together, gradually working in enough warm water to make a pliable dough. Cover with a damp cloth and leave to rest in a warm place overnight.

2 Knock back the dough, then sprinkle the chives over and work them into the dough. Divide into four pieces and flatten each one into an oval or round shape about 3cm (1¼in) thick.

3 Divide the beetroot equally among the four breads, pressing the dice in firmly. Place on a greased baking tray, cover with a damp cloth, and leave to rise in a warm place for 1–2 hours until nearly doubled in size.

4 Preheat the oven to 230°C fan (250°C/highest gas mark).

5 Bake the breads for 25–30 minutes until risen and golden brown. Transfer to a wire rack to cool.

When I first made this bread it was such a hit that it's on all my restaurant menus now. Bin that bread machine you got for Christmas, though, and make this by hand. The result is so much better.

PUMPKIN AND MARJORAM BREAD

makes 1 loaf

1 medium pumpkin
olive oil
salt and pepper
400g (14oz) strong white
  bread flour
100g (3½oz) wholemeal flour
1 tbsp salt
50g (1¾oz) soft butter
30g (1oz) fresh yeast
200ml warm water
2 tbsp roughly chopped fresh
  marjoram

1 Preheat the oven to 200°C fan (220°C/gas 7).

2 Peel the pumpkin, remove the central fibres and seeds, and cut the flesh into cubes. Place in a roasting tin, drizzle with olive oil, and season with salt and pepper. Roast for 45–50 minutes until tender. Remove from the oven and allow to cool. (You need about 250g/9oz cooked pumpkin for the bread.)

3 Meanwhile, put the white and wholemeal flours, salt, and butter in a large bowl. Cream the yeast with a little of the warm water, then add to the bowl. Mix together, gradually adding the rest of the water to make a pliable dough.

4 Turn the dough onto a floured surface. Knead for 5 minutes until smooth. Place in a clean, oiled bowl, cover with a damp cloth, and leave in a warm place for 1 hour until well risen.

5 Roll the dough on a floured surface into a sausage shape, then flatten it. Spread the cooked pumpkin pieces over the dough, pressing them in lightly. Sprinkle with the marjoram, then roll up from a long side like a swiss roll.

6 Place the bread on a lightly greased baking tray, cover with a damp cloth, and leave in a warm place for about 1 hour until well risen and nearly doubled in size.

7 Preheat the oven to 220°C fan (240°C/gas 9).

8 Bake the loaf for 30–35 minutes until golden brown. Transfer to a wire rack to cool.

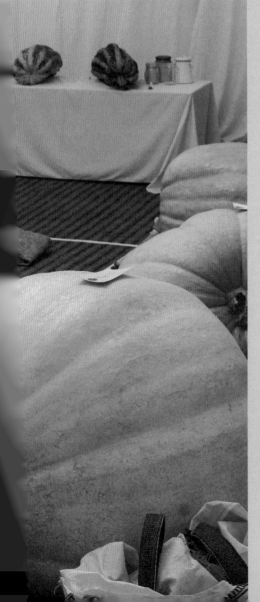

The winning pumpkin at The Great British Village Show weighed in at 405.80 kilos (892.13oz) and required seven army lads to lift it!

When it comes to the monster-sized vegetable categories, performance on the scales is everything. Pumpkins can grow up to 900 pounds, as much as four heavy-weight boxers or one racehorse!

THE HEAVIEST PUMPKIN

Judge Gerald Treweek

"To grow an enormous pumpkin, you must start by obtaining the variety of seed that will enable you to grow a giant. Look out for Atlantic Giant (see pages 216–217).

Start your seeds individually in 18cm (7 in) pots at 85°F. To obtain this temperature without a propagator I use the airing cupboard. Put each pot in a plastic bag with ventilation holes. After three days examine them morning and night. They should germinate by the fifth day. Once they do, bring them into a position of good light and keep them at a minimum of 70°F.

Pumpkins are gross feeders. Prepare a plot of ground 4 yards square and cover to a depth of 1 foot with manure. Plant out the young pumpkin in the middle of the plot and erect a wind break around it. Once the plant is growing away strongly, water it copiously every day. The plant will need feeding once a week. Initially use a high nitrogen feed and then, once the pumpkins start to form, a high phosphate. Finish with a high potash feed for the last month or so up to the show.

When the pumpkins are the size of small melons, remove all but the best two. Let them both grow for a week or so, then select the healthiest one and remove the other. If any other pumpkins form, they must all be cut off. In strong sunlight you must protect the pumpkin by providing some shade, otherwise the skin will harden and could split."

6

chutneys, jams, and jellies

I serve this in my bistros with thin slices of air-dried ham and chargrilled bread, and with salads. It has quite a strong flavour, so you only need a small amount. I use figs, but the same recipe will work with all dried fruit.

DRIED FIG CHUTNEY

makes about 1 litre (1¾ pints)

4 tbsp olive oil
100g (3½ oz) walnuts, roughly chopped
1 tsp finely chopped fresh rosemary
200g (7oz) sultanas
100g (3½oz) raisins
100g (3½oz) Demerara sugar or coconut sugar
400ml (14fl oz) cider vinegar
100g (3½oz) crystallized ginger, finely sliced
675g (1½lb) dried figs, cut in half
1 tsp sea salt
1 tsp freshly grated nutmeg
2 tsp ground allspice

1 Heat the oil in a large saucepan and fry the walnuts until golden. Add the rosemary, sultanas, raisins, and sugar and fry until the fruit begins to caramelize.

2 Pour in the vinegar, bring to the boil, and boil on a high heat for 3 minutes. Add 250ml (8fl oz) water and bring back to the boil, then add the rest of the ingredients. Turn the heat down to a simmer and cook until most of the liquid has evaporated.

3 Spoon the chutney into sterilized jars, filling them as full as you can, and seal while hot. When cold, store in the fridge. If unopened, the chutney can be kept for up to 3 months.

tip Because of the dried fruit, this chutney has a tendency to stick to the bottom of the pan, so keep an eye on it during cooking and stir it well.

Dark-skinned plums give this chutney a beautiful purple-red colour. The reason why plums are good for jams and chutneys is that they are rich in pectin, which is what sets the mixture.

PLUM CHUTNEY

makes about 350g (12oz)

500g (1lb 2oz) dark red plums
2 shallots, chopped
1 tbsp olive oil
100ml (3½fl oz) white wine
  vinegar
1 cinnamon stick
100g (3½oz) Demerara sugar

1 Cut the plums in half down the crease, twist the halves in opposite directions, and pull apart. Prise out the stones and discard. Roughly chop the flesh.

2 Place the chopped shallots in a heavy saucepan with the oil and heat until sizzling. Sauté gently for 5 minutes until the shallots are softened.

3 Add the plums, vinegar, cinnamon, sugar, and 3 tbsp water. Stir until the sugar has dissolved, then simmer, stirring from time to time, for about 15 minutes until the plums are soft and the mixture is slightly thickened.

4 Spoon the chutney into sterilized jars. Seal and leave to cool completely, then store in the fridge. If unopened, the chutney can be kept for up to 3 months.

tip   Jars can be sterilized in the dishwasher (with no soap).

This is my favourite chutney recipe. It's perfect with cheese (try it with the Yorkshire rarebit on page 48) and also goes well with pan-fried cod or salmon.

TOMATO AND APPLE CHUTNEY

fills 2 medium kilner jars

570ml (19fl oz) malt vinegar
450g (1lb) brown sugar
300g (10½ oz) sultanas
15g (½ oz) fresh ginger
3 red chillies, chopped
2kg (4½ lb) tomatoes, roughly
   chopped
500g (1lb 2oz) apples, such as
   Granny Smith or Cox's,
   peeled, cored, and chopped
400g (14oz) shallots, roughly
   chopped
salt and pepper

1 Put the vinegar and sugar in a large pan and bring to the boil, then boil to reduce a little. Add the sultanas and continue to reduce down until the mixture starts to caramelize.

2 Add all the other ingredients and bring back to the boil. Cook, stirring all the time, for 20–30 minutes until thick. The chutney should be chunky, not cooked down to a purée.

3 Allow to cool, then pack the chutney into sterilized jars and seal. Store in the fridge. If unopened, the chutney can be kept for up to 3 months.

Phil Vowles competed in the heaviest marrow and heaviest pumpkin classes at the Dyffryn Gardens Great British Village Show, and here is his chutney recipe — great for using up a glut of marrows.

PHIL VOWLES'S MARROW CHUTNEY

makes about 4 x 450g (1lb) jars

1.35kg (3lb) marrow, peeled
  and seeded
salt
225g (8oz) shallots, sliced
225g (8oz) apples, peeled,
  cored, and sliced
225g (8oz) sultanas
225g (8oz) Demerara sugar
900ml (1½ pints) malt vinegar
12 black peppercorns
2cm (¾in) piece dried whole
  root ginger

1 Cut the marrow into small pieces, place in a bowl, and sprinkle liberally with salt. Cover and leave for 12 hours.

2 Rinse and drain the marrow, then place in a pan with the shallots, apples, sultanas, sugar, and malt vinegar. Tie the peppercorns and ginger in muslin and place in the pan. Bring to the boil, then reduce the heat and simmer, stirring from time to time, until the consistency is thick, with no excess liquid.

3 Pot in sterilized jars or bottles, cover, and label.

One of the most crowd-pleasing and hotly contested classes at The Great British Village Show was the heaviest marrow and the winning marrow at the final weighed in at an astounding 44.8 kilos (98lbs 10oz).

Head Judge Medwyn Williams advises, "To grow any of the giant vegetables, be they the longest or heaviest, the prerequisite is for the right strain of seed; you simply can't make a silk purse from a sow's ear". (See pages 216–217 for recommended varieties.)

THE HEAVIEST MARROW

Head Judge Medwyn Williams

"Germinate marrow seeds on a few layers of wet kitchen tissue in a container, cover with more wet tissues and close the lid. Place the receptacle in a warm room, an airing cupboard is ideal, and after about three days, check them daily. Once the radicle is starting to emerge from the seed case, you will have broken the seeds's dormancy. Pot on in compost using a 7.5cm (3 in) pot and then a 15cm (6 in) pot. Plant out when the weather has warmed up but protect them with a temporary polythene structure or tall barn-type cloches."

Judge John Trim

"The marrow needs plenty of room to develop on a plot rich in manure. As the main stem grows, peg it down to the soil and cover lightly with soil to encourage further root growth. When the main stem reaches the outer limit of the growing space, train it back towards the main plant. Select two or three marrows to grow on the main stem. Reduce them to one if you want a real whopper."

Judge Gerald Treweek

"Feed marrows with a high nitrogen soluble feed when the fruits have set. But be careful not to overfeed as they could go soft and split."

Ross Keightley at The Great British Village Show at Montacute House

This piquant chutney only needs to be kept for a few days before you can eat it, but the courgettes will get softer the longer you leave it.

COURGETTE CHUTNEY

makes about 500g (1lb 2oz)

2 small lemons
3 medium courgettes
2 onions, thinly sliced
100ml (3½fl oz) dry white wine
2 tsp brown sugar
24 black peppercorns, coarsely crushed
2.5cm (1in) piece fresh ginger, peeled and finely chopped
sea salt

1 Peel the lemons, cutting away all the pith, then slice them thinly and discard the pips.

2 Cut the courgettes lengthways in half and then across into 2.5cm (1in) pieces.

3 Combine all the ingredients in a saucepan, adding a little sea salt. Cover and cook over a moderate heat for 1 hour, stirring from time to time. There will be quite a bit of liquid at the end of the cooking time, but once the chutney has cooled, the consistency will be perfect.

4 Allow to cool, then pack into sterilized jars and seal. Keep in the fridge for 4–5 days before serving. If unopened, the chutney can be kept for up to 3 months.

The Great British Village Show
Nostell Priory, West Yorkshire

This majestic 18th-century stately home made a welcome setting for the regional heat in Yorkshire. After months of tending their vegetable plots, honing their recipes, and sourcing the best ingredients, entrants battled with nerves as they made the finishing touches on the showbenches. The competitive spirit was high as the judges, with decades of experience between them, tasted, measured, and weighed, scrutinized, inspected, and examined the produce in the search for the regional winners to go forward to the final at Highgrove. All the judging of the vegetables was done according to the National Vegetable Society Judges' Guide.

I really love fruit chutneys. I don't know whether it's the smell of them cooking or the anticipation of them in the jars, just waiting for you to try them.

GOOSEBERRY AND GREEN PEPPERCORN CHUTNEY

makes about 900g (2lb)

600g (1lb 5oz) fresh green or
   red gooseberries
2 onions, chopped
1 garlic clove, crushed
½ tsp mustard powder
1 tsp lemon juice
300ml (10fl oz) cider vinegar
   or white wine vinegar
175g (6oz) raisins
good pinch of salt
125–150g (4½–5oz) soft
   brown sugar
2 tbsp green peppercorns in
   brine, drained

1 Put the gooseberries, onions, garlic, mustard, and lemon juice in a large pan and pour over two-thirds of the vinegar. Bring to the boil, then reduce the heat and simmer, stirring occasionally, for about 45 minutes until thick. During cooking, add 2 tbsp water if necessary.

2 Add the raisins, salt, sugar, and the rest of the vinegar. Stir over a low heat until the sugar has dissolved, then simmer, stirring frequently, for 45 minutes to 1 hour until thick and syrupy. Stir in the peppercorns, then remove from the heat.

3 Either leave to cool, then pack into jars and store in the refrigerator for up to a month, or pour immediately into hot sterilized jars, seal, and store in a cool, dark place. If unopened, the chutney can be kept for up to 3 months.

For me, this is far better than the bought stuff. I've started to make it with green tomatoes too. It's a great way of enjoying the fresh tomato flavour from the summer over the winter — with chips, of course.

HOME-MADE TOMATO KETCHUP

makes about 500ml (17fl oz)

250ml (8fl oz) cider vinegar
½ tsp ground coriander
½ tsp ground cinnamon
8 tbsp Demerara sugar
1.5kg (3lb 3oz) ripe tomatoes, quartered and deseeded (weight after preparation)
1 bay leaf
1 tsp salt
1 tbsp mustard powder
1 garlic clove, crushed
2 tbsp tomato purée
Tabasco sauce to taste

1 Place the vinegar, coriander, cinnamon, and sugar in a heavy pan and bring to a simmer. Add the tomatoes and all the other ingredients. Bring to the boil, stirring to prevent any sticking. Once up to the boil, reduce the heat and simmer, stirring most of the time, for 30 minutes. Be careful the ketchup doesn't catch and burn on the bottom of the pan.

2 Discard the bay leaf. Blitz the ketchup in a food processor or blender, then push through a sieve. Allow to cool, then pour into sterilized bottles or jars and seal. Keep in the fridge. If unopened, the ketchup can be kept for up to 3 months.

tip   If the ketchup is too thin once cold, bring it back to the boil and stir in a little cornflour mixed to a paste with water, to thicken.

All you need to make a perfect jam is fresh berries, sugar, and a little lemon. The golden rule is: don't overcook the jam or it will lose its fresh fruit taste.

CHUNKY STRAWBERRY JAM

fills 1 medium kilner jar

600g (1lb 5oz) preserving sugar
grated zest and juice of
  1 lemon
1kg (2¼lb) fresh strawberries,
  hulled and cut in half if large

1 Put the sugar, lemon zest and juice, and 3 tbsp cold water in a large pan and heat slowly until the sugar has dissolved.

2 Add the strawberries and stir gently. Bring to the boil and cook for 3–4 minutes, or up to 10 minutes if you prefer a thicker-style jam, stirring occasionally.

3 Remove from the heat and leave to cool slightly, skimming off any froth with a clean spoon. Spoon the jam into a sterilized jar and seal. Store in the fridge. If unopened, the jam can be kept for up to 3 months.

Alison Landels competed at Wimpole Hall and this is her winning recipe. She says, "Strawberry jam is one of the hardest jams to make – this year I made three lots and they all came out differently. You must try not to overcook it or you will lose the good colour".

ALISON LANDELS'S STRAWBERRY JAM

1.35kg (3lb) strawberries
6 tbsp fresh lemon juice
1.35kg (3lb) jam sugar with
 added pectin

1 Hull the strawberries. I chop them into small pieces as my family don't like large pieces of strawberry in the jam; or you can mash them roughly with a potato masher. Put the strawberries into a preserving pan, add the lemon juice, and simmer gently for about 20 minutes (do not boil).

2 Add the sugar and continue to cook gently until sugar has dissolved. Bring to the boil and boil rapidly until setting point is reached – about 25 minutes. To test, remove the pan from the heat, place a little of the jam onto a cold saucer, and allow to cool. If you can then push your finger through, making a wrinkle, you have reached setting point.

3 When the jam is ready, remove the pan from the heat and skim off the skin from the surface. At this point I put six clean jam jars in the oven to heat up. Leave the jam to stand for 10 minutes, then stir thoroughly to distribute the fruit evenly.

4 Pour into the sterilized jars. Cover and label.

tip If the next day you don't have a good set, put it all back in the pan with another 225g (8oz) sugar and the juice of 1 lemon, gently heat it to boiling point, and boil for 20 minutes. Then pot into clean jars.

Whether you like it chunky or smooth, thick or runny, strawberry jam is a British classic that perfectly captures the taste of summer. The Great British Village Show judges were looking for a delicious flavour and good consistency. Presentation rules were strict, with points available for the jar, the label, and the seal.

THE STRAWBERRY JAM CLASS

Judge Beryl Village
"If the fruit isn't good enough to eat fresh, it's not going to make first-class jam. Always choose first-class fruit."

Judge Lyn Blackburn
"For jam making, strawberries should be fresh, clean, dry, and slightly under-ripe."

Judge Lyn Blackburn
"Because strawberries are low in pectin, instead of using granulated sugar, use jam sugar or preserving sugar. They contain natural pectin and citric acid that help to set the jam."

Judge Beryl Village
"To test the jam, remove it from the heat, take a cold saucer from the fridge and spoon a small amount of jam onto it. Leave the jam until it is cold. If the jam has wrinkled, it is ready to pot. If not, return the jam to the heat and continue cooking."

Daphne Neville at The Great British
Village Show at Montacute House

It was the Romans who were first thought to have served mint and other herb sauces with cooked meats. I've added pineapple to this mint jelly, but you can also use apple. This goes well with lamb and chicken.

MINT AND PINEAPPLE JELLY

makes about 650g (1½lb)

3 leaves of gelatine
150ml (5fl oz) cider vinegar
25g (scant 1oz) sugar
pinch of salt
25–30g (1oz) fresh mint,
  finely shredded
1 pineapple, peeled
  and chopped

1 Soak the gelatine leaves in cold water for 4–5 minutes to soften, then remove from the water and set aside.

2 Gently heat the vinegar, sugar, salt, mint, and 4 tbsp water in a pan until the sugar has dissolved. Remove from the heat.

3 Sauté the pineapple pieces in a saucepan until soft, without colouring. Purée the pineapple in a food processor and transfer to a bowl. Stir the softened gelatine into the warm purée until dissolved, then add the mint mixture and stir well.

4 Allow to cool and set (ideally overnight) before serving. The jelly can be kept in the fridge for up to a week.

There is always a jam competition at any village show around the country, and this recipe would be a winner. There is no real secret to this other than using great fruit bang in season and full of flavour.

RASPBERRY JAM

fills 1 kilner jar

450g (1lb) caster sugar
900g (2lb) fresh raspberries

1 Preheat the oven to 150°C fan (170°C/gas 3).

2 Spread the sugar on a baking tray and warm in the oven.

3 Tip the sugar into a heavy pan and add the raspberries and 100ml (3½fl oz) water. Place a sugar thermometer in the pan. Bring to the boil and reduce down over a high heat until the temperature reaches 104°C.

4 Remove from the heat and allow to cool for about 5 minutes. Skim off the froth.

5 Pack into warm sterilized jars and cover with greaseproof paper tops. Keep in the fridge or a cold larder for up to a week.

tip   To test for set without a thermometer, put a spoonful of jam on a chilled saucer and allow to cool, then push the jam with your finger.

Audrey Broad was the winner of the strawberry jam class at the Petworth Great British Village Show. This is another of her recipes, which is an excellent accompaniment to cheese and biscuits.

AUDREY BROAD'S QUINCE JELLY

1.8kg (4lb) quinces
sugar

1 Wash and chop the quinces. Place in a pan with 2.4 litres (4 pints) of water. Bring to the boil, then reduce the heat and cover the pan. Simmer the fruit for about 1 hour until it is reduced to a pulp. Pour into a jelly bag set over a bowl and leave to drain for 10–15 minutes.

2 Set the bowl of juice aside. Replace the pulp from the jelly bag in the pan and add 1.2 litres (2 pints) water. Simmer the pulp for a further 30 minutes before draining it again.

3 Combine both batches of juice and measure the yield. Then test it for setting. Weigh out 350–550g (12oz–1¼lb) of sugar for each 600ml (1 pint) of juice, depending on the pectin content.

4 Pour the juice into a clean pan and bring to the boil. Reduce it by boiling if necessary. Add the sugar and stir until it has dissolved. Bring back to a full boil and boil hard until setting point is reached.

5 Pour the jelly into sterilized jars, cover, and label.

Adding herbs gives a slightly different flavour from the norm. but rosemary is great in jam just like thyme in apple sauce. Trust me, it works.

DRIED APRICOT AND ROSEMARY JAM

fills 2 medium kilner jars

450g (1lb) caster sugar
900g (2lb) dried apricots,
   roughly chopped
2 sprigs of fresh rosemary,
   chopped

1 Preheat the oven to 150°C fan (170°C/gas 3).

2 Spread the sugar on a baking tray and warm in the oven.

3 Meanwhile, put the apricots and 250ml (8fl oz) water in a heavy pan and warm slowly on a low heat until the fruit starts to soften. Tip in the warmed sugar and stir well. Place a sugar thermometer in the pan. Bring to the boil and reduce down over a high heat until the temperature reaches 104°C.

4 Remove the pan from the heat and allow the jam to cool for about 20 minutes.

5 Stir in the rosemary. Pack into warm sterilized jars and cover. Keep in the fridge for at least a week before eating. If unopened, the jam can be kept for up to 3 months.

RECOMMENDED VARIETIES

There are so many varieties of fruit and vegetable you can grow, and it can be confusing to know which to choose and where to start. So here are some recommendations – for the showbench and for the kitchen – from The Great British Village Show judges Gerald Treweek, John Trim, and Medwyn Williams.

APPLES

Ashmeads Kernal An old Russet apple of superb quality, invariably comes top in independent taste tests
Bramley Has stood the test of time as the most reliable apple for cooking and baking
Cox Mouthwatering and probably the nation's favourite eating apple
Devon Crisp A sweet, juicy, shiny red eating apple with high yields
Egremont Russet Has a wonderful nutty flavour
Howgate Wonder A culinary apple, has large fruits of good quality and is an excellent keeper
Jester Recent A new introduction, red in colour with a terrific flavour; this apple tree is ideal for the domestic garden
Jumbo Very good for baking
Self Fertile Queen Cox A self-fertile variety, which means there's no need for a pollinator
Worcester Pearmain Has a sweet strawberry flavour

ASPARAGUS

Argenteuil A 19th-century heirloom French variety with purple spears
Backlim Has a very sweet flavour and good disease resistance
Connovers Colossal An old favourite, with thick spears
Crimson Pacific Has purple spears
Gijnlim A new, all male variety with excellent flavour that was a consistent top performer in recent European trials by out-yielding others by 25 per cent
Mary Washington An old favourite

from North America
Millennium (F1) Has a great flavour

BEETROOT

Boltardy John's standby – an older and cheaper variety that still wins prizes on the showbench and is excellent for eating
Cheltenham Green Top A long-rooted variety with tender flesh
Crimson Globe Great for roasting
Cylindra Long, slim variety
Kestrel (F1) Harvest as a baby beet for pickling or boiling and serving cold in salads
Pablo (F1) RHS Award of Merit 2005 – Medwyn's choice for an exhibition globe beetroot; this has dark crimson flesh
Red Ace (F1) John's top F1 choice, this is probably the most consistent show winner
Solo Good exhibition variety

BROAD BEANS

Bunyards Exhibition John's best all-rounder
Green Windsor, White Windsor John's best beans for flavour
Masterpiece A long-podded variety with very tender, green seeds
Optica A low growing plant – a good choice if your garden is exposed to the elements
Relon, Hylon Long-podded varieties, ideal for competition
Stereo Mangetout-type bean with excellent flavour; as it has few beans it is ideal for cooking whole
The Sutton Dwarf A variety with six to eight beans per pod

BROCCOLI

Claret (F1) Thick-speared British-bred variety – the world's first F1 hybrid
Red Arrow (F1) John's first choice, a purple variety of excellent quality
Summer Purple Excellent colour
White Star Produces high quality white spears

CABBAGE

April (F1) (spring heading and early summer maturing) Compact, dark green pointed heads with uniform habit – ideal for the small garden
Autoro (summer-autumn variety) John's first choice for exhibition in the red class; also an excellent cabbage for pickling
Brunswick This is the heaviest class

of giant cabbage – you'll need a wheelbarrow to fetch this one from your vegetable plot
Celtic, January King (winter maturing) Excellent traditional varieties that stand well without splitting
Hispi (F1), Classic (F1), Charmant Sweet-flavoured varieties
Ormskirk A savoy-type cabbage that can be harvested over a long period
Pyramid (F1) (spring heading and early summer maturing) An outstanding cabbage for quality greens, very reliable and consistent
Ramco (summer-autumn) This is a certain winner on the showbench in the white cabbage class
Squadron (F1) (winter maturing) A new variety that has excellent long-term storage capabilities

CALABRESE

Arcadia John's top choice
Green Comet A good second choice, and easier to find than Arcadia
Green Magic (F1), Ironman (F1) These have a vigourous growing habit and make head production that much easier

CARROTS

Chantenay Red Cored No. 2 Gerald's best-tasting carrot of all
Chantenay, Tip Top, Autumn King John's top choices for flavour
Flyaway (F1), Resistafly Medwyn's choice for the best carrot-fly resistance
New Red Intermediate (red skinned) The outstanding variety in the long carrot class
Parmex A round variety that Medwyn calls the "Golf ball carrot"
Purple Haze (purple skinned), **Nutri Red** (red skinned), **Rainbow (F1)** (assorted colour skins) All will look great at Sunday dinner
Trevor (F1), Cybele (F1) Top choices for a stump rooted carrot

CAULIFLOWER

Aviso (F1) Top variety and winner of RHS Award of Merit
Beauty (F1) First choice for the showbench and the kitchen
Cornell (F1) Newer hybrid, winning regularly at most shows
Deakin (F1) Well-wrapped curds with a late autumn harvest
Fargo (F1) An exhibition variety with deep white curds

Mayflower, Primo (F1) Sow these in October for harvesting in May and June

Memphis, Liberty, Minneapolis, Lateman Good exhibition varieties

Nautilus (F1) Exhibition variety with solid heavy curds

CELERY

Celebrity Has very little stringiness (self-blanching)

Crystal, Loretta, Victoria Front runners of the self-blanching type

Evening Star, Morning Star, Red Star, Starburst New hybrids of the trench type; superb quality for the showbench or the kitchen

Ideal Gerald's best celery of all

Turners White An exhibition variety with crisp, white sticks

CHICORY

Apollo Compact variety – good for steaming or blanching for salads

Brussels Whitloof The traditional forced variety that is good blanched and used in salads

Herb Chicory Roots Can be baked and used to make ersatz coffee

Sugar Loaf (Pain De Sucre) Resembles a well-grown Cos lettuce and stands for a long period

COURGETTES

Bambino (F1) An early variety with dark green baby fruit and heavy yields

Cora (F1) John's top choice for exhibition; has good uniformity

Elite (F1) Green fruits and heavy yields

One Ball (F1), Eight Ball (F1) New round varieties to try if you want to be different

Solcil, (F1), Taxi (F1), Orelia (F1) Good yellow fruits

Tosca (F1), Defender (F1) Good second choices to Cora, with dark green fruits

Zuchini The best open pollinated variety that wins lots of prizes

FIGS

Brown Turkey Widely grown in Britain and has sweet succulent fruit; is best grown against a wall as it prefers a little more warmth

Rouge de Bordeaux An excellent choice for flavour if you have a greenhouse

Violetta Frost-hardy variety that fruits up to 115g (4oz)

White Marseilles Widely grown in Britain; tolerates the cold and can be grown as a bush, but roots must be contained, otherwise they will take over the garden

KALE

Black Tuscany Has very dark leaves

Dwarf Green Curled Gerald's top choice for flavour

Red Russian A fast-growing variety

Redbor Has red-tinged leaves that are good in salads – it was perfect for Head Judge Medwyn's Chelsea displays with the curly foliage and crimson tinged veining adding a softening effect to it

Westland Winter A good cropper

LEEKS

Cumbrian A pot leek that regularly wins at the highest level

Julian (F1), Jolant, Mussleburgh, Prenora Mild-flavoured varieties

Lyon, Prize Taker, Snowdon (F1) John's favourite varieties for the kitchen

Peter Clark selection, Welsh Seeding In Medwyn's view, best for exhibition, usually grown from pips or bulbils, which are available from specialist seed catalogues

ONIONS

Centurion Is easy to grow and can be planted straight into the soil from sets in spring

Hytech Has a long storage life and great flavour

Kelsae The onion to grow if you want to stage them in the large onion class at shows; large onions tend to be milder than their smaller cousins and are excellent raw in salads or sandwiches

Marco (F1) A high-yield exhibition variety, mild flavour and bright skin

Red Baron Has a deep blood-red colour and is a favourite culinary main-crop onion; keeps well, is easy to grow, and can be planted straight into the soil from sets in spring

Senshyu Semi-Globe Yellow and Buffalo Japanese-type onions for seed sowing or sets from late August to mid September, to be ready for harvesting from early June, thereby filling the gap until regular onions are ready

Tasco A globe-shaped variety with beautiful bronze skin and a strong flavour; high yielding and a regular winner on the showbench

PARSNIPS

Albion, Javelin, Princess, Duchess New hybrid varieties to look out for

Archer (F1) A javelin-shaped exhibition variety

Gladiator (F1) The first ever F1 hybrid and the one to grow if you want to win on the showbench

Lancer, Javelin Good for exhibiting and excellent for eating too

Merlin Good Large exhibition variety with very white skin

Tender and True Gerald's best tasting variety

PEARS

Concorde Self-fertile variety

Conference Longish fruits, best picked in September and stored

Doyenne du Comice John's first choice, a very large juicy pear that has outstanding flavour combined with ease of cultivation

Invincible Crisp and juicy when first picked; very hardy

Red Williams An early, easy-to-grow variety with uniform red sheen when ripe; for picking from late August

PEAS

Early Onward A good, reliable variety – the best all-rounder

Greenshaft A good early with an abundance of pods in pairs

Hurst Green Shaft A heavy cropper, with eight to ten peas per pod

Jaguar Double-podded heavy cropper

Kelvedon Wonder An early variety and John's top pea for flavour

Show Perfection The exhibition variety to grow if you want to win

Sugar Snap Tall plants with very sweet-tasting peas

POTATOES

Axona, Mira Currently the only two registered blight-resistant maincrop varieties

Catriona Introduced in 1920; makes the most delicious roast potatoes

Kestrel John's banker, great to eat and a winner for the exhibition table too – a beautiful part-blue oval/long second early potato

Lady Christl, Sharpes Express Medwyn's favourites, old and trusted, with bags of taste

Maxine An all-red exhibition variety with superb smooth skin

Nadine An early exhibition variety

with strong overall disease resistance
Picasso An exhibition variety with rosy pink eyes
Pink Fir Apple A chef's favourite for salads
Red Duke of York, Rocket Early croppers with heavy yields
Winston A top choice for the white class in competition – has been unbeatable; unfortunately rather low in dry matter and consequently lacks flavour if grown to maturity

PUMPKINS

Atlantic Giant The huge variety used for exhibitions
Baby Bear A trailing miniature pumpkin with orange fruits; good for eating
Ghost Rider 6–9kg (13–19lb), **Gold Fever** 6–8kg (13–18lb), **Harvest Moon** 6–8kg (13–18lb), **Jack O'Lantern** 4–5kg (9–11lb), **Jack of All Trades** 5–7kg (11–15lb), **Rebecca (F1)**, **Pie Star** 3–4kg (6–9lb), **Small Sugar** 2–3kg (4–6lb) All good for eating, especially Rebecca and Pie Star
Snowman A white variety, suitable for painting

RADISHES

China Rose A large variety with rose-coloured skin, ideal for salads and cooking
French Breakfast A fast-growing, bi-coloured variety with great taste and long crunch
Jolly (F1) A high-quality, cherry-belle type that is good for eating
Long White Icicle Fairly hot, sweet white radish that matures quickly
Marabelle A very early variety with round, bright red roots
Prinz Rotin A big radish – great for the showbench

RASPBERRIES

Autumn Bliss An outstanding choice for lots of quality fruit
Glen Ample, Glen Magna Very heavy croppers with superb flavour
Glen May Produces large fruits that can be picked from the end of June
Himbo Top, Joan J Show-winners with large size and good flavour
Malling Jewel An old favourite that has excellent flavour
Malling Minerva An early variety – replaced the popular Glen May in many cases because of better disease resistance

Octavia A first-class later-season variety

RHUBARB

Gaskins Perpetual All year round
Harbinger An old variety with a very deep colour
Stockbridge Arrow An impressive exhibition variety with a thick stem
Timperley Early Another top exhibition variety that should be picked young
Victoria An old favourite that is very crisp with a strong rhubarb flavour

RUNNER BEANS

Butler Has very fleshy pods and is fairly stringless
Encima Exhibition A variety with long, straight pods
Hestia Dwarf A runner that works well in containers
Lady Di A stringless bean with high-quality pods
Liberty, Enorma-Elite Worthy contenders on the showbench; also good in the kitchen, provided they are picked young
Polestar Stringless early cropper
Prizewinner The most prolific runners John has ever grown
Red Rum A very vigorous variety
Stenner Strain An almost invincible show winner

SHALLOTS

Ambition Has some success on the showbench, but the main advantage is its low price
Aristocrat, Hative de Niort Top exhibition varieties that often win and are excellent to eat too
Jermor A new exhibition variety with a mild flavour; a chef's choice
Red Sun Good spicy flavour
Topper Great for pickling

SPINACH

Bloomsdale A deep green leaved variety that is easy to grow and known for its resistance to bolting
Bordeaux A new variety with unique Christmas tree shaped leaves
Medania A high-yielding variety that can be sown to crop in either summer or winter
Palco (F1) A large thick leaved variety that has good resistance to bolting
Perpetual Spinach A leaf beet; John recommends it if you find real spinach too strong in flavour

Reddy (F1) Has a sweet flavour and dark red stems
Scenic (F1) The first variety to be fully resistant to Downy Mildew; very high yielding and full-flavoured with a high nutrient content

STRAWBERRIES

Alice, Hapil, Symphony Good mid-season choices
Aromel A great perpetual berry
Florence A late cropper with dark red, firm fruit
Mae An early cropper with large, firm, sweet fruits that you can pick outdoors from early June or even from mid May if you give the plants a little protection
Marshmallow An excellent cropper
Rosie A good early-fruiting choice
Royal Sovereign Has superb flavour
Sonata A good late-season choice; has conical fruit

TOMATOES

Cedrico (F1) An exhibition variety with uniform fruits
Gold Star An outstanding show variety
Goliath A beefsteak tomato with great flavour
Piccolo For Medwyn, these have the most superior tomato taste
Shirley (F1) An older exhibition variety that still gives newer varieties a run for their money, and has real flavour
Tropical Ruby (F1) For Gerald, these are the sweetest tasting tomatoes
Tumbler (F1) Ideal in hanging baskets
Vanessa (F1) An exhibition variety with a long shelf life

RESOURCES DIRECTORY

MEAT, POULTRY, AND GAME

Ark Chicken Company, The
www.arkchicken.co.uk
Babylon Lane, Silverton, Exeter,
Devon EX5 4DT
Tel/Fax: 01392 860460
Email: info@arkchicken.co.uk
Traditional free-range poultry from
slow growing breeds, including
chicken, geese, turkey, quail, and
corn-fed guinea fowl; the birds
are housed in moveable arks (also
available for sale), which means they
can be regularly moved on to fresh
pasture.

Boathouse Organics
www.boathouseorganicfarmshop.co.uk
The Orchards, Uckfield Road, Clay Hill,
Lewes, East Sussex BN8 5RX
Tel: 01273 814188
Email: infoboathouseorganicfarmshop.co.uk
Award-winning Soil Association
organic meat.

Brown Cow Organics
www.browncoworganics.co.uk
Perridge Farm, Pilton, Shepton Mallet,
Somerset BA4 4EW
Tel: 01749 890298
Email: enquiries@browncoworganics.co.uk
Four times winner at the Organic
Food Awards. Specialises in beef
products.

Colin M. Robinson
www.britnett-carver.co.uk/robinsonsbutchers
41 Main Street, Grassington, Skipton
Tel: 01756 752476 Fax: 01756 753985
An award-winning family butcher
and retailer of the superb Limestone
Country Beef. Deliveries direct to your
door.

Dartmoor Happy Hogs
www.moorlandsfarmshop.co.uk
Moorlands Farm Shop, Whiddon Down,
Okehampton EX20 2QL
Tel/Fax: 01647 231666
Award-winning sausages, home-
cured hams and bacon. Available to
buy online.

Derbyshire Smokery
(Alan and Barbara Hobson)
www.derbyshiresmokery.co.uk
Greystones, Ashbourne Road, Flagg,
Derbyshire SK17 9QQ
Tel/Fax: 01298 83595 Email:
alanandbarbara@derbyshiresmokery.
co.uk
Aromatic and fragrant home smoked
meats and fish. Contact directly for
wholesale orders or visit them at
Derbyshire's food markets.

Eversfield Organic
www.eversfieldorganic.co.uk
Ellacott Barton, Bratton Clovelly,
Okehampton EX20 4LB
Tel: 01837 871400 Fax: 01837 871114
Email: sales@eversfieldorganic.co.uk
Has a unique herd of "Heritage"
Aberdeen Angus. Organic lamb, pork,
pheasant, and poultry is also born
and reared on the farm.

Farmhouse Pantry, The
(Richard Gill and family)
1 Barnes Lane, Dronfield, Woodhouse,
Derbyshire S18 8YE
Tel: 01246 298 123 or 07890 433 674
The only UK stockists of Peak District
water buffalo.

Fletchers of Auchtermuchty
www.seriouslygoodvenison.co.uk
Reediehill Deer Farm, Auchtermuchty,
Fife KY14 7HS
Tel: 01337 828369 Fax: 01337 827001
Email: info@fletcherscotland.co.uk
Highly regarded suppliers of venison.
Available by mail order or from their
farm shop.

Greenfield Pork Products
(Martin Martindale)
Sunnycliff, Highbury Road, Anna Valley,
Andover, Hampshire SP11 7LU
Tel/Fax: 01264 359422
Email: martinanddawn@greenfield.
pork.co.uk
High welfare free-range pork products.
Range of pork cuts, sausages, bacon
and gammon, and a comprehensive
hog-roasting service.

G Scott of York Ltd.
www.scottsofyork.co.uk
81 Low Petergate, York,
North Yorkshire Y01 7HY
Tel: 01904 622972
Rare breeds of British beef, lamb, and
pork. Orders can be made online.

Higher Hacknell Farm
www.higherhacknell.co.uk
Burrington, Umberleigh, Devon EX37 9LX
Tel/Fax: 01769 560909
Email: info@higherhacknell.co.uk
A full range of award-winning organic
meats that can be delivered direct to
your door.

Laverstoke Park Farm
Overton, Hampshire RG25 3DR
Tel: 01256 772820 Fax: 01256 772809
Email: farmshop@laverstokepark.co.uk
Organic meat, poultry, and eggs from
rare breeds reared slowly. Available
by mail order.

Longwood Farm
www.longwoodfarm.co.uk
Tuddenham, St. Mary, Bury St. Edmunds,
Suffolk IP28 6TB
Tel/Fax: 01638 717120
Email: longwoodorganics@hotmail.com
Produces a variety of organic meats
including beef, lamb, pork, poultry,
sausages, and bacon. The farmshop
stocks a range of organic goods.

Old Smokehouse, The
www.the-old-smokehouse.co.uk
Brougham Hall, Brougham, Penrith,
Cumbria CA10 2DE
Tel/Fax: 01768 867772
Email: sales@the-old-smokehouse.co.uk
High quality gourmet smoked foods,
including local fish and meat.

Park Hill Farm
www.parkhillfarm.co.uk
Hales, Market Drayton,
Shropshire TF9 2QA
Tel/Fax: 01630 652178
Email: beef@parkhillfarm.co.uk
Produces traditionally reared, mature
British beef. Meat can be bought
online or by phone.

Swillington Organic Farm
(Jo Cartwright)
www.swillingtonorganicfarm.co.uk
Garden Cottage, Coach Road,
Swillington, Leeds LS26 8QA
Tel: 07974 026076/0113 2869129
Fax: 01132 869129
Email: jo@swillingtonorganicfarm.co.uk
Award-winning organic pork, lamb,
beef, and chicken, all available by
mail order.

West Country Ostrich
www.westcountryostrich.co.uk

Crinacott Farm, Pyworthy, Holsworthy, Devon EX22 6LJ
Tel: 01409 253 401 Fax: 01409 254 555
Email: sales@westcountryostrich.co.uk
Ostrich steaks, sausages, ham, oak-smoked ostrich, pasties, and pies.

FISH
Arbroath Smokies
(Iain Spink)
www.arbroathsmokies.net
Forehills Farmhouse, Carmyllie
nr. Arbroath, Angus
Tel: 01349 884169/01241 860303
Traditionally-made Arbroath smokies, smoked over hardwood. Freshly hot smoked haddock and trout are available at farmers' markets, fairs, and agricultural shows around Scotland.

Cockleford Trout Farm
Cowley, Cheltenham, Gloucestershire GL53 9NW
Tel: 01242 870325
Email: clare@cockleford.wanadoo.co.uk
A family-run trout farm.

Creelers
www.creelers.co.uk
Brodick, Isle of Arran KA27 8DD
Tel: 01770 302797 Fax: 01770 302810
Email: sales@creelers.co.uk
A family-run restaurant and smokehouse that produces home-cured and smoked fish and shellfish.

Derbyshire Smokery
(see previous page)

Maldon Oysters and Seafood Co.
www.maldonoyster.com
Birchwood Farm, Cock Clarks, Chelmsford, Essex CM3 6RF
Tel: 01621 828699 Fax: 01621 828944
Email: sales@maldonoyster.com
Oysters and shellfish, wet fish, and smoked fish sold direct.

Norfolk Kipper House
www.norfolkkipperhouse.co.uk
56 Pine Grove, Sheringham, Norfolk NR26 8QS
Tel: 01263 820320
Fresh and smoked seafood, pastes, and pates available from farmers' markets and Richard's fish shop in Sheringham. Their speciality is potted shrimp, which is available to buy online.

Old Smokehouse, The
(see previous page)

Purely Organic
www.purelyorganic.co.uk
Deverill Trout Farm, Lonsbridge, Deverill, Warminster, Wiltshire BA12 7DZ
Tel: 01985 841093
Email: mail@purelyorganic.co.uk
Specialises in organic trout, but also sells fruit, vegetables, meat, poultry, dairy, and bread.

FRUIT AND VEGETABLES
Abel and Cole Ltd.
www.abel-cole.co.uk
8-15 MGI Estate, Milkwood Road, London SE24 0JF
Tel: 08452 626262
Fresh organic fruit and veg, organic meat and sustainably sourced fish, most from UK farms. Runs a very popular box scheme.

Blackmoor Nuseries
www.blackmoor.co.uk
Blackmoor Farm Shop, Blackmoor Liss, Hampshire GU33 6BS
Tel: 01420 473782 Fax: 01420 475878
Email: blackmoor.farmshop@virgin.net
The farm shop specialises in fresh fruit and sells a wide variety of locally grown vegetables, homemade cakes, bread, and cider.

Cassons English Herbs
www.cassonsenglishherbs.com
Frith Farm, Wheathold, Tadley, Hampshire RG26 5SA
Tel: 01189 819755
Sell high quality fresh herbs and herb products. Produce ranges from teas and honeys to confectionary and dressings.

Charlton Orchards
Charlton Road, Creech St. Michael, Taunton, Somerset TA3 5PF
Tel: 01823 412959
Email: sally@charlton-orchards.co.uk
Grows traditional varieties of fruit. Available from the farm shop, online, or by mail order.

Chegworth Valley Juices
www.chegworthvalley.com
Water Lane Farm, Chegworth, Harrietsham, Kent ME17 1DE
Tel: 01622 859272 Fax: 01622 850918

Hand-selected, farm pressed apple and pear juices. Can be bought online for home delivery.

Dragon Orchard
www.dragonorchard.co.uk
Dragon House, Putley, Ledbury, Herefordshire HR8 2RG
Tel: 01531 670071
Email: info@dragonorchard.co.uk
Fine apples from traditional orchards.

Garlic Farm, The
www.thegarlicfarm.co.uk
Newchurch, Isle of Wight PO36 0NR
Tel: 01983 865378 Fax: 01983 862294
Email: web@thegarlicfarm.co.uk
The UK's premier grower of garlic and source of garlic products. Products available to buy online and at farmers' markets nationwide.

Harroway Organic Gardens
www.thewhitchurchweb.org/business/harroway
Kingsclere Road, Whitchurch RG28 7QB
Tel: 01256 895346
Email: hogveg@hotmail.com
Grows fruit and vegetables and runs a local box scheme.

Hayles Fruit Farm
www.hayles-fruit-farm.co.uk
Winchcombe, Cheltenham, Gloucestershire GL54 5PB
Tel: 01242 602123 Fax: 01242 603320
Email: info@hayles-fruit-farm.co.uk
Farm and orchard producing apples, pears, and other fruit. Produce available from the farm shop, website, and local farmers' markets.

Hope Organic Produce
Hope House, Sandy Lane, Stoke Heath, Shropshire TF9 2LG
Tel: 01630 638348
Email: sue@hopeorganicproduce.co.uk
Has held a Soil Association certificate for 15 years. Grows plants and vegetables.

Isle of Wight Tomatoes
www.isleofwighttomatoes.co.uk
Wright Salads, Main Road, Hale Common, Arreton, Newport, Isle of Wight PO30 3AR
Tel: 01983 866907 Fax: 01983 864679
Email: info@isleofwighttomatoes.co.uk
Specialises in organic tomatoes, sold at farmers' markets throughout the South.

Kingcup Farm
www.kingcupfarm.com
Willetts Lane, Denham UB9 4HE
Tel/Fax: 01895 832865
Email: info@kingcupfarm.co.uk
Supply fresh fruit and vegetable boxes locally for collection from the farm, and sell produce at farmers' markets in the South East, and from their own farm shop.

Linscombe Farm
Newbuildings, Crediton, Devon EX17 4PS
Tel: 01363 84291
Email: info@linscombe.co.uk
300 varieties of vegetables produced throughout the year for supply direct to consumers.

Ogg Valley Organics
www.oggvalleyorganics.co.uk
1 Westfield Farm, Ogbourne St. George, Marlborough, Wiltshire SN8 1SX
Tel: 01672 841373
Email: contact@oggvalleyorganics.co.uk
Farm with an organic dairy herd and a wide range of vegetable and salad crops. Runs a home delivery and veg box scheme and sells through farmers' markets and farm shop.

Perry Court Farm
www.perrycourtfarm.com
Garlinge Green, Canterbury, Kent CT4 5RU
Tel: 01227 732001
Kent's first organic and bio-dynamic farm.

Peter Mushrooms
www.petermushrooms.co.uk
Sandhill Farm, Pickets Hill, Sleadford, Bordon, Hampshire GU35 8TF
Tel: 01420 478366 Fax: 01730 892990
Email: petermushrooms@aol.com
A small independent mushroom farm, specialising in fresh mushrooms, mushroom products, and composts.

Watergull Orchards
(David Fisher)
www.watergullorchards.co.uk
Watergull House, The America, Sutton-in-the-Isle, Ely, Cambridgeshire CB6 2NY
Tel/Fax: 01353 777700
Email: david@watergullorchards.co.uk
Small family-run business that produces over 30 varieties of high quality English apple juice. Online home delivery ordering available.

Weardale Organic Soup Company, The
(Christine Peart)
www.waredalesoup.com
Elm Cottage, Westgate-in-Weardale, Bishop Auckland, Co. Durham DL13 1LP
Tel/Fax: 01388 517384
Email: weardalesoup@aol.com or christine@weardaleorganicsoup.co.uk
Uses artisan production methods and local vegetables to make gluten-free vegetarian and vegan soups. Available from local farmers' markets and by mail order.

DAIRY PRODUCE

Alder Carr Farm
www.aldercarrfarm.co.uk
Creeting St. Mary, Ipswich, Suffolk IP6 8LX
Tel: 01449 720820 Fax: 01449 723777
Email: info@aldercarrfarm.co.uk
Produces celebrated Fruit Cream Ice and sells locally produced food from the farm shop.

Arran's Cheese Shop
www.islandcheese.co.uk
Home Farm, Brodick, Isle of Arran KA27 8DD
Tel: 01770 302788
Email: info@islandcheese.co.uk
Produces delicious cheddars, which can be bought from their shop in Ayr and online.

Cheese Gig, The
(Kathy Gig)
www.thecheesegig.com
Orchard Barn, Buckland St. Mary, Chard, Somerset TA20 3TA
Tel: 01460 234581 Fax: 01460 234501
Email: kath@thecheesegig.com
Purchases can be made direct from their website, or you can become a member and receive discounts on future purchases. A subscription service is also available: Kathy selects four or five cheeses every month and posts them with tasting notes.

Cream O'Galloway Dairy Company Ltd.
www.creamogalloway.co.uk
Rainton, Gatehouse of Fleet, Castle Douglas DG7 2DR
Tel/Fax: 01557 814040
Email: info@creamogalloway.co.uk
Luxury organic ice cream and frozen yoghurt, produced using milk from their own dairy on Rainton Farm for markets in Scotland and South-East England.

Farmer Gosden's Ice Cream
www.farmergosden.co.uk
The Cottage, Goddards Farm, Sherfield-on-Loddon, Basingstoke, Hampshire RG27 0EL
Tel/Fax: 01256 881007
18 flavours of luxury jersey ice cream. On sale in local farm shops, village shops, delicatessens, and farmers' markets. Hampshire Life finalist – Best Newcomer of the Year 2004.

Gundenham Dairy
(John Cottrell)
www.gundenham-dairy.co.uk
North Gundenham, Langford Budville, Wellington, Somerset TA21 0OR
Tel: 01823 662704 Fax: 01823 660239
Core products are milk, cream, yoghurts, and potatoes, which they deliver to individual customers as well as businesses.

Lincolnshire Poacher Cheese
(Simon Jones)
www.lincolnshirepoachercheese.com
F.W. Read and Sons Ltd., Ulceby Grange, Alford, Lincolnshire LN13 0HE
Tel: 01507 466987
Lincolnshire Poacher is a handmade, traditional recipe, unpasteurised cheese made using milk from a herd of 170 Holstein cows between October and May. Available at farmers' markets and a variety of cheese shops and delicatessens.

Neal's Yard Creamery
(Charlie Westhead)
www.nealsyardcreamery.co.uk
Caperthy, Arthurstone Lane, Dorstone nr. Hay on Wye HR3 6AX
Tel/Fax: 01981 500 395
Email: ny.creamery@virgin.net
A small dairy, overlooking the Wye Valley, originally part of Neal's Yard Dairy. Make award-winning fresh and mould-ripened cheeses, yoghurts, and crème fraiche.

Ronaldo Ices
(Rob Ellis)
The Ice Cream Factory, 44, Lothian Street, Norwich NR2 4PH
Tel: 01603 633127
Email: info@ronaldo-ices.co.uk

Uses locally grown ingredients where possible and does not use flavourings or colours.

Smart's Traditional Gloucester Cheese
www.smartsgloucestercheese.com
Old Ley Court, Chapel Lane, Birdwood, Churcham, Gloucester GL2 8AR
Tel: 01452 750225
A family farm, making award-winning traditional handmade Gloucester cheese from unpasteurised cow's milk.

Staffordshire Cheese Company, The
(Adrian Corke)
Glenmore House, 55 Rose Bank, Leek, Staffordshire ST13 6AG
Tel: 01538 399733 or 01538 361919
Fax: 01538 399985
Email: jknox1066@aol.com or leekbrewery@hotmail.com
Produces a variety of handmade cheeses from locally produced milk, which is pasteurised at the farm's own dairy. Cheese can be bought locally through a number of retailers and at 14 local farmers' markets.

Wester Lawrenceton Farm
Forres, Moray IV36 3RH
Tel: 01309 676566
Sweet milk cheese from unpasteurised organic milk of Ayrshire cows. Available at farmers' markets and cheese shops in Scotland.

SWEETS AND PRESERVES
A & M Johnson, Honey & Hive Products
www.hampshirefare.co.uk/johnson
Grasmead, Limekiln Lane, Bishops Waltham, Southampton, Hampshire SO32 1FY
Tel/Fax: 01489 892390
Email: am.johnson@btinternet.com
Beekeeper producing various honeys, marmalades, fudge, candles, and skin creams.

Blackaller Honey
www.blackaller.co.uk
Rosemary Cottage, North Bovey, Devon TQ13 8RA
Tel: 01647 440322
Email: peter@blackaller.fsbusiness.co.uk

Heather and wildflower, clear, and set honeys available, according to season. Available from selected retail outlets and farmers' markets.

Bracken Hill Fine Foods
(Neil and Gill Maycock)
www.brackenhillfinefoods.co.uk
West House Farm, Elvington nr. York, North Yorkshire YO41 4AZ
Tel: 01904 608811 Fax: 01904 607799
Email: info@brackenhillfinefoods.co.uk
Award-winning Yorkshire preserves, handmade the old-fashioned way with local produce.

Chilli Jam Company, The
www.thechillijamcompany.co.uk
Emsworth, Hampshire PO10 7UE
Tel: 01243 375 464
Email: info@thechillijamcompany.co.uk
Handmade from fresh local produce with no artificial additives.

Four Shires Apiaries
(Norman Davis)
Tel: 01793 824591
Email: norman_davis@ntlworld.com
Produces a range of honey, honeycombs, candles, furniture polish, and creams.

Golden Meadow Preserves
(Karen Wigley)
Greencroft Farm, Middleton by Youlgrave, nr. Bakewell, Derbyshire DE45 1LS
Tel: 01629 639229
24 varieties of chutneys and pickles, produced from home-grown and local vegetables.

Mrs Huddleston's Luxury Home-Made Provisions
www.mrshuddleston.com
Tel: 01525 261868
Email: info@mrshuddleston.com
Award-winning fruit conserves, jams, marmalades, English wine jellies, and chutneys. Orders by email or phone.

Pickled Pink Preserves
www.pickledpink.co.uk
189 Woodhouse Lane, Bishop Auckland, Co. Durham DL14 6JT
Tel: 01388 661584
Email: crwfrdjoan@aol.com
Pickles, chutneys, cordials, and sauces handmade by traditional methods with no additives. Products sold direct and from local famers' markets.

Whitfield Farm Organics
www.whitfieldfarmorganics.co.uk
Whitfield Farm, Falfield, Wotton Under Edge, Gloucestershire GL12 8DR
Tel: 01454 261010
Email: jfb@whitfieldfarmorganics.co.uk
Produces organic honey and beef. Home delivery service available via the website.

GARDENING SUPPLIES
Aqua Culture
www.aquaculture-hydroponics.co.uk
Tel: 0845 6445544
The UK's leading hydroponics retailer, selling hydroponic systems, indoor grow lights, grow-room ventilation, growth enhancers, and air pumps.

Border Belles
www.members.lycos.co.uk/borderbelles
Old Branxton Cottages, Innerwick, East Lothain EH42 1QT
Tel: 01368 840325
Email: mail@borderbelles.com
Supplies quality plants from their nursery.

Bordervale Plants
(Claire Jenkins)
www.bordervale.co.uk
Nant-y-deri, Sandy Lane, Ystradowen, Cowbridge, Vale of Glamorgan CF71 7SX
Tel: 01446 774036
Specialises in unusual herbaceous perennials, trees and shrubs, and cottage garden plants.

Gardening and Herbs
(Fiona Harpin)
Ackworth Garden Centre
Barnsley Road, Ackworth, Pontefract, West Yorkshire WF7 7NB
Tel: 01977 612660 Fax: 01877 614629

Keepers Nursery
www.keepers-nursery.co.uk
Gallants Court, East Farleigh, Maidstone, Kent ME15 0LE
Tel: 01622 726465 Fax: 0870 7052145
A leading specialist fruit tree nursery with over 600 varieties, from varieties of apple, pear, and plum to more unusual fruit trees such as quince, medlar, and mulberry.

Medwyn's Seeds
www.medwynsofanglesey.co.uk
Llanor, Ffordd Hen Ysgol, Llanfairpwllgwygyll, Anglesey LL61 5RZ

Email: shop@medwynsofanglesey.co.uk
A vegetable and seed specialist and gold medal winner at the Chelsea Flower Show. All seeds available to buy online.

N. A. Kay's Horticultural Products
www.kaysdiscountgarden.co.uk
Unit 10, Snockycar Industrial Estate, Hensingham, Whitehaven, Cumbria CA28 8PF
Tel: 01946 692134 Fax: 01946 691573
Specialist suppliers of gardening products.

Rising Sun Nurseries
www.risingsunnurseries.co.uk
Harrowbarrow, Callington, Cornwall
Tel: 01579 351231
A plant and garden centre that also attends Holsworthy and Tavistock farmers' markets.

Select Seeds
www.selectseeds.co.uk
58 Bentinck Road, Shuttlewood,

Chesterfield S44 6RQ
Tel: 01246 826011
Email: sales@selectseeds.co.uk
Supplies seeds for exhibition and competition.

Selsley Herb Nursery
www.selsleyherbs.co.uk
Hayhedge Lane, Bisley, Stroud, Gloucestershire GL6 7AN
Tel: 01452 770073
Email: rob@selseyherbs.fsnet.co.uk
A small specialist nursery offering a wide range of culinary and medicinal herbs.

COOKING EQUIPMENT
Alan Silverwood Ltd.
www.alansilverwood.co.uk
Ledsam House, Ledsam Street, Birmingham B16 8DN
Tel: 0121 4543571 Fax: 0121 4546749
Email: sales@alan-silverwood.co.uk
Manufacturer of high quality domestic bakeware. Products are

widely available through cookshops, department stores, and online. List of distributors available online.

Divertimenti
www.divertimenti.co.uk
33-34 Marylebone High Street, London W1U 4PT
Tel: 020 7935 0689
and 227-229 Brompton Road, London SW3 2EP
Tel: 020 7581 8065
Email: marylebone@divertimenti.co.uk
or brompton@divertimenti.co.uk

Just Preserving
www.justpreserving.co.uk
8 Church Street, North Walsham, Norfolk NR28 9DA
Tel: 01692 405 777 Fax: 01692 407 855
Email: info@headcook.co.uk
Sells preserving equipment online, such as preserving pans, jars, muslin, and wax discs.

INDEX

Page numbers in **bold** refer to illustrations

James Martin's Acknowledgements
I would like to say a big 'thank you' to the BBC people who made the made the TV series happen
– Elaine Bedell, Peter Fincham, Jay Hunt, and Alison Kirkham – for their belief in me and giving me
a shot. I enjoyed working with all the TV production team at 12 Yard, and would also like to thank my
co-presenters, Alan Titchmarsh and Angelica Bell, and the three brilliant judges – John Trim, Gerald
Treweek, and Medwyn Williams – for their contributions: a great team of people to spend the summer
with at all the amazing country shows. Thanks also go to Pippa Bull, Lisa Harrison, and Chris Start
who help me bring my ideas to life in my kitchen at home. To the ever-patient team at DK – Stephanie
Jackson, Gillian Roberts, Adèle Hayward, Elizabeth Watson, and Sara Robin – you're all stars and
have made this book happen, and I thank you. You get the best food shots courtesy of photographer
Simon Wheeler – another great book mate, thanks to your skills, and you're quick – no messing
about! Finally, thanks to Fiona Lindsay, Linda Shanks, Mary Bekhait, and Alison Lindsay, who make
sure there is never a free day in my diary, but also never a dull moment! Cheers everyone!

Publisher's Acknowledgements
Dorling Kindersley would like to thank the following: Simon Wheeler for photography; Jonathan
Brunton, the photographer's assistant; Chris Start and Lisa Harrison, chef and home economist, for
preparing and presenting recipes for camera; Penny Markham, the prop stylist; Mike Beale, Danielle
Heathcote, and Julianne Turner at 12 Yard Productions; Daniel Mirzoeff at the BBC; Ariane Durkin for
editorial assistance; Laura Nickoll for proofreading and Patricia Carroll for the index.

Picture Credits
All photography © Simon Wheeler, except: © 12 Yard (photographer Ken McKay) 13, 24, 25, 36, 37,
39, 63, 89, 129, 138, 139, 155, 164, 165, 183, 191, 199, 202, 203, 209; © 12 Yard (photographer Neil
Genower) 94, 95; © Nick Ayliffe 41, 109, 179, 221.